EDUCATION IN SAUDI ARABIA

Rewritten and revised by
Hamad I. Al Salloom Ph.D.

Edited by
Ghazy A. Al Makky, Ph.D.

Assistant Editor
Alfred S. Go

Second Edition
1415 AH/1995 AD

Library of Congress Cataloging-in-Publication Data

Education in Saudi Arabia edited by the Relations Department of the Saudi Arabian Cultural Mission to the U.S.A. 2nd edition rewritten and revised by Hamad I. Al Salloom, Ph.D. and Ghazy A. Al Makky, Ph.D. Assistant editor - Alfred S. Go.
    p. 112 cm. 22 x 1/2 x 15
    Includes bibliographical references (p. 4).
    ISBN 0-915957-20-5
I. Education—Saudi Arabia. I. Sallūm, Ḥamad ibn Ibrāhīm.
II. Saudi Arabia. Saudi Arabian Cultural Mission to the United States. Relations Dept.
LA1436.2.E38 1994
370' .538—dc20   94-39197
                                                                                 CIP

Copyright © 1991 by The Saudi Arabian Cultural Mission to the United States. All rights reserved.

Permission must be obtained from the publisher in writing before any part of this work may be reproduced or transmitted in any form or by any means, electronic or mechanical, including photocopying and recording, or by any information storage or retrieval system.

Printed in the United States of America

10 9 8 7 6 5 4 3 2 1

ISBN 0-915957-20-5

amana publications
10710 Tucker Street, Suite B
Beltsville, MD 20705-2223 USA
Tel: (301) 595-5777 Fax: (301) 595-5888

TABLE OF CONTENTS

I. INTRODUCTION 1

II. BRIEF HISTORY OF SAUDI ARABIA 3

III. HISTORICAL DEVELOPMENT OF EDUCATION
IN SAUDI ARABIA 7

    A. Early Education in the Arabian Peninsula 7
    B. King Abdulaziz's Vision and Legacy 9
    C. The Kingdom at the Threshold of
       Modernization 10

IV. OVERVIEW OF THE SAUDI ARABIAN
EDUCATION SYSTEM 15

    A. National Education Policy 15
    B. Features of the Education System 19
    C. Government Agencies Involved in the
       Education System 22

V. DESCRIPTION OF LEVELS OF EDUCATION IN
SAUDI ARABIA 27

    1. Pre-First Level - Kindergarten 29
    2. First Level - Primary (Elementary) 31
    3. Second Level - Intermediate 35
    4. Third Level - Secondary 39
       a) Regular Secondary 41
       b) Modern Secondary 41

      c) Vocational and Technical Secondary 46
    5. Fourth Level - Higher Education 62

VI.   TEACHER TRAINING 77

VII. SPECIAL EDUCATION 83

VIII. ADULT AND EVENING EDUCATION 91

IX.   OTHER TRAINING PROGRAMS 94

X.   CURRICULUM DEVELOPMENT 99

XI.   CONCLUSION 103

XII. SELECTED BIBLIOGRAPHY 104

I. INTRODUCTION

Islam teaches that the pursuit of knowledge is a religious duty for every Muslim. In accordance with this belief, the Kingdom of Saudi Arabia has, over the last seventy years (since 1925), developed a comprehensive educational system that adapts modern educational theories and methods to the needs of a rapidly developing Islamic society.

This book was prepared by the Saudi Arabian Cultural Mission for non-Saudi readers — primarily Western readers, especially educators and students — and offers a concise overview of the Saudi educational system. Our objective is to provide summarized, but authoritative, information inasmuch as the material presently available in English does not discuss specific features of the Saudi educational system or its programs. Our goal is to present a realistic report that addresses the kinds of questions about education the Mission most often receives and make available, perhaps for the first time, data previously confined to studies written in Arabic.

Rewritten and revised, this second edition provides a brief history of the Kingdom of Saudi Arabia as framework for a better understanding of an education system that is unique to Saudi Arabia. It also provides a historical development of education in the Kingdom including a description of the education system, the national educational policy, general purpose of education, the objectives of Islam in achieving the purpose of education, and the regulatory government agencies involved in education. Furthermore, it describes the different levels of education and furnishes insight to subject matters such as special, vocational, technical, adult and evening education, teacher training, and curriculum development with the latest data and newest innovations undertaken in the Kingdom.

In preparing this edition, the Saudi Arabian Cultural Mission in Washington, D.C. hopes to provide a much needed resource for those interested in contemporary education in Saudi Arabia. We hope that readers will write to us with their comments or questions as future editions will respond to such input. This book on education is part of a series of publications that will include volumes on culture, social affairs and science in Saudi Arabia.

We gratefully acknowledge H.R.H Prince Bandar Ibn Sultan, Ambassador of the Kingdom of Saudi Arabia to the United States, whose support made this work possible.

                                  Hamad I. Al Salloom, Ph.D.
                                  Cultural Attache to the United States

II. BRIEF HISTORY OF SAUDI ARABIA

The Royal Kingdom of Saudi Arabia, as we know it today, occupies almost four-fifths of the Arabian Peninsula. Prior to 1902, however, Saudi Arabia consisted of many districts and sheikdoms often described by historians as "a host of petty princelings who contended with each other for power" (Shakhis, p. 4, 5). The roots of the present Saudi polity date back to the eighteenth century when Shaikh Mohammad Ibn Abd Al-Wahhab, after being persecuted and eventually expelled from his native town of Ayaina in 1742, settled in Diriyah. (Sahabi, p. 6) Shaikh Mohammad Ibn Abd Al-Wahhab had called for the return of Muslims to the traditional form of Islam. He was received favorably by Muhammad Ibn Saud, the ruler of Diriyah. Recognizing the need for uniting the tribal groups in the area, the two men subsequently struck an alliance that marked the rise of the House of Al Saud. This relationship flourished and was made even stronger through intermarriage such as the marriage of Mohammed Ibn Saud to the daughter of Shaikh Mohammad Ibn Abd Al-Wahhab. (Rashid and Shaheen, 1987, p. 7)

By the early 1800s, the Al-Saud family ruled much of the Arabian Peninsula. This rise to power alarmed the Ottoman government, which sent forth its armies to contain the influence of Al-Saud. The Ottomans ultimately captured Diriyah, thus ending the first phase of the Al-Saud reign in 1818.

In 1824, the Al-Saud family regained political control of central Arabia. However, after 1865 during a period of unrest, a rival family, the Al-Rashid, extended their power over the Saudi state. The Al-Saud, under the leadership of Abdul Rahman, were forced into exile in 1891.

In 1901, twenty-one year old Abdulaziz Bin Abdul Rahman Al Saud, a direct descendant of Imam Mohammed Ibn Saud and one of the daughters of Shaikh Mohammad Ibn Abd Al Wahhab, left Kuwait determined to recapture all the territory once held by his forefathers and to extend his protection over the holy cities of Makkah and Madinah. In a daring battle, he recaptured Riyadh in 1902 —which marked the beginning of the modern state of Saudi Arabia. The following decades saw Abdulaziz Ibn Abdul Rahman Al Saud unifying the different regions into one nation with Riyadh as its capital.

On September 23, 1932, Royal Decree No. 2716 was issued proclaiming the country as the Kingdom of Saudi Arabia. It was established as an Islamic state, with Arabic designated as the national language and the "Shari'ah" (Islamic law rooted in the Qur'an) and the teachings of the Prophet Muhammad-as its constitution (Taibah, p. 3).

Prior to 1932, the country was very poor with the annual pilgrimage to Makkah as its main source of income. In 1933 an agreement with Standard Oil of California regarding exploration and extraction of oil led to its discovery in commercial quantities in 1938, which sparked the Kingdom's modern development.

Vast oil revenues provided the Kingdom with the financial means for development and with it afforded a new dimension in its role of prominence in the Arab/Islamic region as well as the rest of the world. With development comes change and "....to Saudi leaders and planners, the heritage of the country as the cradle of Islam requires that change, both social and economic, should be pursued in accordance with the teachings of Islam" (Taibah, p. 5).

The Kingdom owes much of its half-century of stability to the legacy of its legendary founder, King Abdulaziz Ibn Saud. He was a remarkable leader of imagination and vision who launched Saudi Arabia from an isolated and little-known country and placed it on the road toward becoming a force with which to be reckoned. He was described as "... a giant of a man in his achievements and strong leadership, enhanced by a majestic physique and warm personality". During his rule, King Abdulaziz laid the foundations for the modernization of Saudi Arabia, building the country's infrastructure and later introducing modern technology, health care, agriculture, but more importantly improving education.

The first institutions of higher education were opened in Makkah, the College of Shariah in 1949 and the Teachers' College in 1957, followed by the Shariah College established in Riyadh in 1953. His legacy of a modern Saudi Arabia, instilled with a strong sense of heritage and tradition deeply rooted in Islam, was passed on to his sons: King Saud, King Faisal, King Khalid, the present King Fahd, Crown Prince Abdullah and Prince Sultan.

King Saud ascended to the throne upon his father's death in 1953. In his twenties, King Saud led many campaigns in the battles to further unite the Kingdom. During his reign, attempts were made on the Kingdom's infrastructure such as the erection of hospitals, schools and the improvement of Hajj facilities. Some of the prominent contributions from his governance were the institution of the Council of Ministers, and the establishment of the Ministries of Education, Health, Commerce, Defense, Foreign Affairs and Telecommunications. Also, King Saud made the first trip by a Saudi monarch to the United States in 1957. It was also during this period that government-sponsored Saudi students were sent abroad. In 1962, Saudi Arabia sponsored an international Islamic conference, which fostered the World Muslim League, headquartered in Makkah.

In 1964 upon the abdication of King Saud due to health reasons, Faisal Ibn Abdul Aziz became king. King Faisal's governance was marked by a respect for tradition combined with innovation. While King Abdul Aziz had shaped the Kingdom, King Faisal built and consolidated it. Having developed extensive experience in foreign affairs at an early age, he devoted great effort to this area during his reign. King Faisal was a central force behind the establishment of the Organization of Islamic Conference (OIC) in Jeddah in 1971 which is composed of Islamic countries and is dedicated to promoting Islamic unity and cooperation. But more importantly, King Faisal is best remembered for initiating the Kingdom's highly successful five-year development plans.

In 1975, King Khalid succeeded King Faisal after his death. Under King Khalid, Saudi Arabia continued its second and third five-year development plans at a remarkable pace and all the country's major infrastructures were established between 1975-1980. During this period, the standard of living increased substantially and the Kingdom achieved political and economic prominence both regionally and internationally. The Gulf Cooperation Council (GCC) was formed in 1981 which linked the Kingdom with its neighboring countries such as Bahrain, Kuwait, Oman, Qatar, and the United Arab Emirates for economic and security cooperation and coordination.

The Kingdom's current monarch, King Fahd Ibn Abdul Aziz, succeeded King Khalid in 1982 after his death. Prior to his ascension to the crown, King Fahd held important government posts such as Minister of Education in 1953, Minister of the Interior in 1962, Second Deputy Prime Minister in 1967 and in 1975 he was the First Deputy Prime Minister. As a prominent leader in the international arena, King Fahd has visited the heads of most of the world's industrialized nations and has affirmed Saudi Arabia's unique position in the Islamic world. His 1981 proposal to resolve the Arab-Israeli conflict secured his prominence in the realm of foreign affairs.

Regionally, King Fahd has helped to achieve reconciliation among Arab as well as other Islamic nations, particularly through the Organization of Islamic Conference and other Islamic forums. He has also guided the country's contributions to the Islamic Development Fund and the Islamic Development Bank. King Fahd played an important role in organizing the GCC, and has helped to guide the Council's efforts to promote peace and stability in the Arabian Gulf region. Also, he has affirmed the Kingdom's position as a leader in the Organization of Petroleum Exporting

Countries (OPEC). And most importantly, he is focused on building enduring prosperity in the Kingdom through the five-year development plans that stress meticulous planning, broad educational opportunities, a diversified economy, resource conservation and an abiding commitment to Islam.

As Custodian of the Two Holy Mosques (Makkah and Madinah), King Fahd, along with the other Saudi leaders, has greatly expanded the facilities at the holy sites and others across the Kingdom. Today, more than two million pilgrims take part in the annual "hajj" (pilgrimage). In 1984, the Kingdom inaugurated a project that expanded the capacity of the Prophet's Mosque in Madinah to accommodate approximately 455,000 worshippers from the initial capacity of 28,000. The capacity of the Holy Mosque at Makkah was also enlarged to accommodate over one million worshippers.

In view of the Kingdom's economic growth and tremendous development in various areas, King Fahd enacted three Royal Decrees that called for a renewal of allegiance to the great bases on which the Kingdom of Saudi Arabia was established. These issued Royal Decrees covered the following: 1) Basic system of government, 2) The Council of Ministers System, and 3) The Shura Council System. King Fahd is confident that these statutes, founded on the customs and traditions of the Saudi people and adhering to Islam, shall, with Allah's help, assist the state in realizing all aspirations of the Saudi citizen, including progress for his homeland and the Islamic nation.

Next in line to the crown is Prince Abdullah Bin Abdul Aziz who became Crown Prince and Deputy Prime Minister in 1982 and has been the commander of the National Guard since 1962. He has actively participated in the government of the Kingdom of Saudi Arabia and has contributed to the consolidation of the Kingdom's position as a moderator and arbitrator in regional politics.

Following in succession to Prince Abdullah is Prince Sultan Ibn Abdul Aziz who has been the second Deputy Prime Minister since 1982 and Minister of Defense and Aviation since 1962. He has helped build and modernize the Kingdom's armed forces and has also contributed to the development of the world class status of the national carrier, Saudi Airlines.

III. HISTORICAL DEVELOPMENT OF EDUCATION IN SAUDI ARABIA

A. EARLY EDUCATION IN THE ARABIAN PENINSULA

Historically, education began very early in the Arabian Peninsula. Education is, in fact, "synonymous with religious teachings ... as our Prophet Mohammad (Peace be upon Him) was the first teacher, the Qur'an the first textbook, and the mosque our first school; and ... is supported by the fact that the (Holy) Qur'an started off with the divine command—Read". (Fozen, p. 1) "... Verses in the *Holy Qur'an* ... state that *talab al-'ilm* (seeking knowledge) is obligatory for every Muslim male and female, and that one must seek knowledge from cradle to grave" (Fozan p. 1). This heritage of Islamic belief laid the foundation for education during the periods in Arabian Peninsula and later for modern Saudi Arabia.

During the first century of Islam (7th century A.D.), in the Al Hijaz which included the cities of Makkah (formerly known as Mecca), Madinah and Jeddah, the most basic form of education was acquired in small schools called the "khuttabs" and were presided over by the preacher or old wise man of the mosque, referred to as the "Imam" . These small schools were located either near or in the mosques and were the precursors of modern elementary schools. Certain areas in Saudi Arabia had two kinds of khuttabs: one exclusively for boys and the other strictly for girls. In other areas of the country, there were khuttabs that allowed coeducation of boys and girls until the pre-Kindergarten age of 6, especially in the western region of Makkah, Jeddah and Madinah. The mosques not only provided a center for worship, but also for learning, discussion and community life in general.

Education, in those early days, meant rote memorization of the Holy Qur'an with secondary emphasis on reading and writing. As mentioned earlier, the khuttabs were open to both boys and girls up to a certain age at which point both could read verses in the Qur'an. The boys usually continued their learning in the khuttab to about the age of 12 by which time they would have memorized the Holy Qur'an, while the girls were confined to education at home, if possible (Dayil, p. 3). Few extended their schooling beyond this level. Those who did prolong their formal education generally pursued specialized instruction in the mosques that were strictly limited to the Islamic science curriculum of *Hadith* (prophetic traditions), *Tafsir* (exegesis of the Qur'an and Hadith), *Shar'ia* (Islamic creed), *Fiqh* (Islamic jurisprudence), and *Fara'id* (obligations).

Education existed but did not flourish during the Turkish Rule. Religious training was conducted in the two holy Mosques at Makkah and Madinah. A census taken in 1883 in the Al-Hijaz area, conducted in the Turkish language, described only two formal kinds of education, governmental and private. The centralized governmental education consisted of three years elementary education followed by a "Rushdiah" stage which included three years of schooling, a prerequisite to the next level or preparatory stage. The curriculum included history, Arabic, geography, French, art, physical education, Arabic poetry and the Qur'an. The language of instruction was Turkish. Aside from the government schools, there were industrial, agricultural and teacher education schools.

These schools were not popular with the Arabic people for two reasons: 1) they were afraid of the effects the Turkish language would have on their children; and 2) they were afraid that education in these schools would result in enlistment in the Turkish Army. (Khateeb, p. 80)

Because the khuttabs offered only the most basic type of training, it was recognized that there was a need for a more advanced education similar to the Turkish governmental education but without any of its influence. Consequently, some wealthy local citizens and concerned Muslims from India and other Muslim nations provided funds to organize a form of private school. In 1875 the Solateyah School was founded with approximately 200 students and 10 teachers. Tuition was free and the curriculum was generally academic in content and included Qur'anic studies. The school levels were: 1) four years of preparatory; 2) four years of elementary; 3) four years of secondary; and 4) two years of higher education. About 25 subjects were taught in this school with emphasis on students' abilities. Other well known schools in Makkah during that period were the Fakriah, the Kaireah and the Falah schools. Aside from these were 12 other schools located in Medina, all patterned similarly to that of the Solateah School. All these schools were closed in 1961.

B. KING ABDULAZIZ'S VISION AND LEGACY

Education has been one of the first and most prominent benefits accompanying the development of the modern Saudi state. King Abdulaziz understood the importance of education in enlightening and unifying a diverse population. In 1925, the Directorate of Education was established, a year before issuing the Basic Instructions that laid the foundation for a centralized national system of government. Egyptian assistance was called upon to initiate an educational system patterned after the Egyptian system which had French origin. This system provided for a six year elementary followed by a five year secondary cycle. (Towagry, p. 8)

The educational policy as outlined in Article 23 of the Basic Instructions in 1925 stated that "while strictly observing the teachings of religion, education should cover the dissemination of knowledge and the opening of schools. The policy also provided instructions for the protection of the institutes of learning all over the Kingdom. With the establishment of the Directorate of Education in 1925 came the founding of the first government-supported post-elementary school in the Kingdom, the Al-Ilmi Institute, a religious institute.

The first Education Council was formed by King Abdul Aziz in 1928 and consisted of eight members, four of whom were government employees and the other four non-government officials. But it was not until March 18, 1938, that the regulations of the General Directorate of Education were announced providing the General Directorate of Education (to have) complete supervision over all the educational affairs in the Kingdom, except for military education. The duties of the General Directorate of Education before the 1950s were mainly the establishment and regulations of schools, as the entire country was in the process of laying the foundation for educational organization. Prior to the establishment of the public school system, only four private elementary schools existed in the Al-Hijaz province, namely: the Assawlatiyyah, the Al-Fakhariyyah, the Al-Authmaniyyah, and the Al-Falah schools in Jeddah and in Makkah which were all placed under the supervision of the Directorate of Education upon its establishment in 1925.

In 1932, the founding of the Kingdom of Saudi Arabia expanded the responsibilities of the Directorate of Education in terms of territory. Many new schools were established; most notably, the Religious Sciences School in 1933 and the Tahdeer Al-Baathat School or Foreign Mission Preparation School, the first secondary school that prepared its graduates for university education abroad in 1935. Other landmarks in educational development included the publication of the first elementary school curriculum in 1934 and the issuance of regulations for private schools in 1937. The objectives of the Directorate of Education were revised in 1937, to pave the way for more than a decade of reform and improvement such as the establishment of the Technical Intermediate School in 1949 A.D.(1369 A.H.) - the first seed of technical education, and the first illiteracy eradication evening school in 1930. The beginnings of higher education in the Kingdom also took root during this period with the establishment of the College of Sharia in Makkah (now known as the Umm Al Qura University) in 1949, the Teachers' College in 1952, the College of Sharia in Riyadh in 1953, and the College of Arabic Language in Riyadh in 1954 (presently a college in the Imam Mohammad Ibn Saud University).

Economic constraints limited the impact of the pioneering efforts of the Directorate of Education in laying the foundation for a modern educational system in Saudi Arabia, especially during World War II. In 1947 the number of schools in the entire Kingdom, from preparatory through the secondary levels, totalled only 65 with a total enrollment of approximately 10,000 male students.

C. A KINGDOM AT THE THRESHOLD OF MODERNIZATION

By the year 1952, there were 306 elementary schools in the Kingdom (Dayil, 1978, p. 3). A 1950 UNESCO publication however estimated the percentage of illiteracy in Saudi Arabia to be 92% to 95% (Fozan, p.4). This figure caused a great deal of concern to the Saudi government. Therefore, a new era in the development of modern education began in 1953 with the establishment of the Ministry of Education on December 24, 1953, (Towagry, 1973, p.8) as part of the Council of Ministers. His Excellency, King Fahd Ibn Abdulaziz was appointed the first Minister of Education and guided the Ministry's unprecedented expansion and modernization of educational resources. With its establishment more schools were opened, and public education started to expand throughout the country. The expansion in education was so rapid that the Ministry of Education found it necessary to create 'school districts' in different parts of the country to assist the Ministry in discharging its responsibility. (Dayil, 1978. p. 5) Each school district was administered by a superintendent with a technical staff. Each school district was responsible for the day-to-day operation of schools under its jurisdiction with overall direction emanating from the Ministry of Education. (Fozan, p. 2)

In 1954, the Ministry of Education established a special department called Popular Culture (Fozan, p. 4) to combat adult illiteracy. It was entrusted with the supervision of all adult evening classes.

In 1958, the Kingdom of Saudi Arabia, along with other members of the Arab League, agreed upon a uniform educational system, that provided for a 6-year elementary, a 3-year intermediate and a 3-year secondary cycle with a separate higher education program. (Towagry, p. 9)

Although verses from the Holy Qur'an state that seeking knowledge is obligatory upon every Muslim male and female, women were excluded from acquiring formal education in the early days until separate schools were established or when families who could afford the private education of their daughters made arrangements for special tutorials conducted at home. It was not until 1961 that girls' education was provided by the Saudi government with the establishment of the General Directorate of Girls' Education.

The opening of the first schools for girls was not without opposition. "There was so much dissension that the National Guard was summoned to restore order." (Hobday, 1978. p. 95) But despite this inauspicious beginning, the General Directorate of Girls' Education established 16 primary schools with 128 classrooms and 148 staff members to serve 5,200 female students.

Aside from the girls' education, the 1960s witnessed a massive effort in the development of higher education as well as the attempt to develop a curriculum that is uniquely Saudi, one that did not rely heavily on the Egyptian secondary school curriculum. This period was characterized by trial and error and reforms in curriculum development.

The seventies coincided with two five-year National Development Plans (1970-1975 and 1975-1980) that stressed a basic philosophy for the successful modernization of the Kingdom of Saudi Arabia. This philosophy was based on two major principles: 1) developing the needed human resources through education and training, and 2) building a comprehensive economic infrastructure. Due to their importance to the National Development Plans, human resources development, along with infrastructure, economic resources and social resources including education, were given high priority. During the first five-year plan, $3 billion was allocated for education. The plan's objective was to increase the overall elementary level enrollment. Intermediate level facilities had to be expanded, especially in the rural area, in order to permit enrollment of all elementary graduates who desired admission. Although enrollment at the secondary level was expected to increase, the plan aimed at admitting only 50 per cent of the intermediate level graduates into general secondary education and at channelling the other 50 per cent into teacher training and vocational/technical programs. With the girls' education, the plan was different. Enrollment of girls was to increase considerably on all levels notably by 95% at the elementary level by 1974.

The 1970s witnessed mammoth development of the infrastructure and an increase in school facilities with the aim of accommodating an enrollment in line with the third and fourth Five-Year Development Plans.

The eighties sought the continuation of human resources development through the improvement of the quality of education, in order to achieve the ultimate objective of 'Saudization' of the workforce.

Some important educational innovations and reforms introduced in the period 1986-1988 are as follows: (Development of Education, 1986-88, p.61)

1) Issuance of a Royal Decree which reorganized the Ministry of Education and led to the creation of the "Directorate General for Educational Technology". The new Directorate, consisting of two departments: "Design Department" and "Production Department" adopted the three following objectives:

   a. to stress the training of the senior staff of the Educational Ministry and Educational Districts in the fields of educational technology, teaching aids and equipment;

   b. to pay more attention to the design and production of educational materials;

   c. to supply all types of advanced educational technology materials to schools, such as films, laboratories, equipments, computers (which was introduced in the newly developed secondary school curriculum). In addition, the Directorate made available video tapes in its main office.

2) gearing the efforts of the Directorate General for Educational Supervision and Training towards raising the standard and efficiency of teachers in educational supervision and to develop a program for Teachers' In-Service training;

3) more decentralization of final exams at the primary school and intermediate school levels through decision of the Higher Committee on Education No. 1640, dated 10/4/1401 and Circular of the Ministry of Education No. 34/3/7, dated 17/5/1408 A.H. (1988 A.D.).

Significant changes which took place in 1990-1992 were: (Development of Education, 1990-1992, pp.45-49)

1) the completion of the English language books, i.e. student's book, teacher's book and activity book in the intermediate level (which are now in use in all schools following a trial period);

2) the phasing out of the credit hour system in the secondary level effective from the First Grade of Secondary level—1990/91;

3) the upgrading of programs in the seventeen Teachers' Colleges to grant a Bachelor's Degree to graduates who completed 149 credit hours over four consecutive years;

4) the implementation of a new curriculum, following a thorough study by the Ministry of Education that takes into consideration learners' inclinations and the reduction of the period of study from four to three years.

5) In Special Education:

—a ministerial order's instruction that no student may be dismissed from any level of education for repeated failure as long as he/she is still in the age bracket of that level;

—establishment of new units and facilities and modernizing existing ones to improve the care and services offered to the handicapped;

—the improvement of curricula for special education;

—the launching of a program at the King Saud University's College of Education to produce teachers specialized in the teaching of the blind, deaf and mentally retarded.

IV. OVERVIEW OF THE SAUDI ARABIAN EDUCATIONAL SYSTEM

A. NATIONAL EDUCATION POLICY

"Seeking knowledge" as viewed in Islam is mandatory for every Muslim, male or female. This mandate is the cornerstone of education in Saudi Arabia. The Islamic character of education is well-defined in the document "Educational Policy in Saudi Arabia" which was written in 1970 by the Higher Committee of Educational Policy and contains a total of 236 articles covering the principles and objectives for all levels of general education.

This comprehensive document serves as the main reference in the formulation of ideas and provides the main principles that direct education, its policies, plans, objectives, aims, systems, curricula, teacher training, and evaluation system. In it, the national education policy states that the "educational process (should) fulfill the duty of acquainting the individual with his God and religion and adjusts his conduct in accordance with the teaching of religion, in fulfillment of the needs of society, and in achievement of the nation's objectives."

Islam is not only integral to Saudi education but also serves as the very essence of its curriculum. This is evident in the following principles of education which state that education should: (Education Policy, pp. 6-9)

1. Strengthen faith in God and Islam, and in Mohammad (Peace be Upon Him) as Prophet and Messenger of God.

2. Foster a holistic, Islamic concept of the universe, man and life, such that the entire world is subject to the laws of God in fulfilling its duty without any interruption or confusion.

3. Emphasize that life is a stage of work and production during which

the Muslim invests his capacities with a full understanding of and faith in the eternal life in the other world. Today is work without judgment and tomorrow is judgment without work.

4. Proclaim that the message of Mohammad (Peace be Upon Him) ensures happiness to man and rescues humanity from all the corruption and misery.

5. Instill the Islamic ideals of a humane, prudent and constructive civilization guided by the message of Mohammad (Peace be Upon Him) to realize glory on earth and happiness in the other world.

6. Engender faith in human dignity as decreed by the Holy Qur'an and that each Muslim is entrusted with the task of fulfilling God's wishes on earth.

7. Reinforce that it is the duty of each Muslim to seek education and the duty of the state to provide education in its various stages within the state's capacity and resources.

8. Incorporate religious education as a basic element in all the primary, intermediary, and secondary stages of education and maintain Islamic culture as a basic course in all the years of higher education.

9. Integrate Islamic orientation in sciences and knowledge in all their forms, items, curricula, writing and teaching so that they would fall in harmony with sound Islamic thinking.

10. Stimulate the use of human knowledge in the light of Islam to raise the standard of living of our country and nation and to fulfill our role in world cultural progress.

11. Foster absolute faith in the fundamentals of the Islamic nation and its unity regardless of race, color and geographical distance.

12. Teach the importance of our national history, the preservation of the heritage of the Islamic religion, and learn from the lives of our ancestors using their experience as a guiding light for our present and future.

13. Promote Islamic solidarity and strengthen cooperation among Islamic peoples in order to protect them against all dangers.

14. Teach respect for the general rights guaranteed by Islam in order to maintain law and order and achieve stability for the Muslim community in its religion, soul, family, honor, mind and property.

15. Advocate social solidarity among the members of the Muslim community through cooperation, love, fraternity and through placing public interest over private interest.

16. Enlighten that God has bestowed a special responsibility on the Kingdom of Saudi Arabia as: a) guardian of Islam's Sacred Places; b) defender of the land in which inspiration descended on Prophet Mohammad (Peace be Upon Him); c) in her adoption of Islam as creed, worship, law, constitution and way of life; and d) in its responsibility of spreading the word and wisdom of Islam throughout humanity.

17. Pronounce that the preaching of Islam throughout the world, with prudence and persuasion, is the duty of the state and its citizens.

18. Inspire strength in its most sublime form—strength of faith, character, and body—because a strong faith is closer to God's heart than a weak faith.

Corollary to the above articles on education policy, Article 28 declares the general purpose of education is "to have the student understand Islam in a correct and comprehensive manner; to plant and spread the Islamic creed; to furnish the student with the values, teachings and ideals of Islam; to equip him with the various skills and knowledge; to develop his conduct in constructive directions; to develop the society economically, socially and culturally; and to prepare the individual to become a useful member in the building of his community."

Articles 29 to 61 of The Education Policy specifies the objectives of Islam in achieving the purpose of education, stressing the cultural and religious role of the Kingdom; most prominent of which are as follows: (Ministry of Education, 1980, pp. 11-12)

1. Promoting the spirit of loyalty to Islamic law by denouncing any system or theory that conflicts with this law and by honest action and behavior in conformity with the general provisions of this law.

2. Demonstrating the full harmony between science and religion in the Islamic law, as Islam is a combination of religion and secularism, and Islamic thought meets all the human needs in their highest forms and in all ages.

3. Encouraging and promoting the spirit of scientific thinking and research, strengthening the faculties of observation and meditation, and enlightening the student about God's miracles in the world and God's wisdom in His creatures; thus enabling the individual to fulfill an active role in building a social life and in steering it toward the right direction.

4. Understanding the environment in all forms, broadening the horizons of students by introducing them to the different parts of the world and the natural resources and products that characterize each country, emphasizing the wealth and raw resources of our country, their geographical location, and economic position. Accepting a leadership role in safeguarding Islam, calling people to accept it, and working for the solidarity of the Islamic world.

5. Furnishing the students with at least one of the living languages, in addition to their original language, to enable them to acquire knowledge, arts and useful inventions, transmit our knowledge and sciences to other communities, and participate in the spreading of Islam and serving humanity.

6. Keeping pace with the characteristics of each phase of the psychological growth of young people, helping the individual to grow spiritually, mentally, emotionally, and socially in a well-rounded way, and emphasizing Islamic spirituality so that it will be the main guideline of private and public behavior for the individual and the society.

7. Studying individual differences among students so as to properly orient them and assist them to grow in-line with their abilities, capabilities and inclinations.

8. Caring for academically retarded students and eliminating as many of their handicaps as possible and setting up special permanent and provisional programs to fit their needs.

9. Training the necessary manpower and diversifying education with special attention to vocational training.

10. Planting the zeal of work in the hearts of students, commending it in all its forms, urging individuals to excel in their work and to emphasize its role in the construction of the nation. This is done by:

   a. Forming scientific skills and attending to applied sciences in school to give the student the chance to practice handicraft activities, participate in production, and acquire experience in laboratories, construction work and farms.

b. Studying the scientific principles of various activities so that the level of mechanical production will attain progress and invention.

11. Awakening the spirit of Islamic struggle to fight ignorance and poverty, resume its glory and fulfill the mission of Islam.

12. Establishing the strong relations that exist among Muslims and protect the unity of the Muslim Nation.

B. FEATURES OF THE EDUCATION SYSTEM

An understanding of education in Saudi Arabia depends largely on an awareness of its special characteristics. While some of these are present in other educational systems, the combination in Saudi Arabia is unique. The special features of the Saudi education system are as follows:

1. *Emphasis on Islam*—The education of the Muslim individual must be in accordance with the primary objective of God: creating human beings to worship Him and to please Him. God says: I have created *Jinn* (devils) and mankind only to worship me. (The Holy Qur'an 51:56) (Baltow, 1983, p. 72).

Islam is not a collection of verses and rituals to be memorized and recited in prayers; it is considered a way of life for the present and future. Therefore, practice and application are vital aspects.

Saudi Arabian education is closely related to the concept of Islamic education as seen in its Educational Policy, general purpose, and objectives with great emphasis on Islam. Islam is the very soul of its curriculum and may best be illustrated by the number of periods per week devoted to the study of the Qur'an, Islamic tradition, jurisprudence, and theology -- from the first level of kindergarten to the last level of higher education. It is, however, important to note that in this respect, religious studies are not taught as separate entities but in their corresponding relation with the other fields of study such as education, economics, sociology, psychology, medicine, and law. The memorization of the Qur'an, interpretation and understanding of the Qur'an (*Tafsir*), and the applications of Islamic tradition to everyday life are veritably stressed.

2. *Centralized Educational System*—The qualities and characteristics of

the national education policy in Saudi Arabia emanate from the external human heritage and the rich Islamic values. While the Supreme Commission on Educational Policies sets basic policy, goals and major structural elements for the national educational system, the Ministry of Education in Riyadh is responsible for providing general education for males in all parts of Saudi Arabia and the General Presidency of Girls' Education is responsible for providing general education for the females. All the educational directorates spread in different parts of the Kingdom follow the same educational policy, curricula, educational hierarchy, evaluation techniques, and methods of instruction as stated by both the Ministry of Education and the General Presidency of Girls' Education. These policies are also employed by the private, non-state sponsored schools and special training schools directed by other government agencies such as the Ministry of Defense and others.

3. *Separate Male and Female Education*—Following the norms of Muslim tradition, but more specifically, as stated in Article 155 of the Educational Policy of Saudi Arabia, there is strict compliance to the separation of the sexes in all levels of education, with the exception of kindergarten and nursery, and some private elementary schools in the first and second grades as well as some medical school classes. It must be understood however, that girls' education in separate institutes is mainly an issue related to the respected social status given to women by Islam. As such, there are separate school buildings and staff and, in some cases, completely separate institutions. At the higher education levels, where necessary, female students listen to lectures from male teachers through the use of closed-circuit television, e.g., in the medical fields. But the curricula are similar for both boys and girls with minor exceptions in physical education and home economics.

4. *State Financial Support*—Realizing that education is the cornerstone for the achievements of the comprehensive national development plans, the Saudi government was and is firmly committed to the development of education at all costs. Furthermore, believing that educating its people is the sole responsibility of the state, education is made available to all who want it, and is free to all Saudi citizens and residents. Although it is free, education is not compulsory (Dayil, 1978, p. 8).

In addition to free tuition, the state provides for various stipends, subsidies and bonuses to students in specific fields of training. Stipends and free housing are provided to all post-secondary students and to those secondary level students who must attend school away from home. Students in all levels of technical and vocational schools also receive stipends. In most cases, meals and transportation are substantially subsidized. Transportation is made available free of charge to female students. The government also provides the students with both preventive and curative medical care, as well as full boarding services in some educational institutions.

The funding of educational institutions, faculty, staff and students is generous and has grown dramatically during the last two decades. Government appropriations for education in 1974-75 totaled approximately 3.8 billion Saudi riyals or approximately $1 billion, while in 1983-84 the total allocation increased to 27.4 billion Saudi riyals or approximately $7.31 billion. The total allocation for education in the Fifth Development Plan (1990-1995) is $26.9 billion or 17.9 percent of government expenditures. Table 1-A below illustrates the allocation for education relative to the Kingdom's entire budget, while Table 1-B shows how this allocation is distributed to the four principal agencies involved in education.

TABLE 1-A
BUDGET ALLOCATION
(IN MILLION SAUDI RIYALS)

ITEM	YEAR	
	(1) 1990/91	1995/96
STATE BUDGET	SR 143,000	SR 150,000
EDUCATION ALLOCATIONS	25,460	26,987
PERCENTAGE RELATIVE TO STATE BUDGET	17.8%	17.9%

(US$1.00 = 3.75 SAUDI RIYALS)

---

(1) Sources: Ministry of Education, 1992, p.50.

TABLE 1-B
DISTRIBUTION OF EDUCATION ALLOCATIONS
(IN MILLION SAUDI RIYALS)

ORGANIZATION	(2) 1403/1404	1415/1416
Ministry of Education	SR 11,367	
Presidency of Girls' Education	5,963	
Ministry of Higher Education	696	
Universities	8,070	
Gen. Organization for Technical Ed & Voc. Training	1,254	
TOTAL	**SR 27,350**	**SR 26,987**

(US$1.00 = 3.75 SAUDI RIYALS)

---

(2) Source: Ministry of Education, 1984-1985, p. 139.

C. GOVERNMENT AGENCIES INVOLVED IN THE EDUCATION SYSTEM

There are four government agencies involved with planning, administrating and implementing the overall governmental educational policy in Saudi Arabia. These are:

—The Ministry of Education.
—The General Presidency of Girls' Education.
—The Ministry of Higher Education.
—The General Organization for Technical Education & Vocational Training.

1. **The Ministry of Education**—The Ministry of Education, was established in 1373 A.H. (1953 A.D.) replacing the Directorate of Education which was functioning under the Ministry of Interior.. The Ministry of Education is presently considered the largest centralized educational agency in Saudi Arabia. Its responsibilities range from policy-making, planning, and budgetary staffing to providing physical and teaching materials and supplies to all elementary, intermediate, and secondary male schools. It is also responsible for adult education, special education and teacher training programs. The Ministry undertakes research and development programs related to the development of curriculum and teaching methods. It is also responsible for the library system, the museums and archeological research that is taking place in Saudi Arabia. Finally, the Ministry represents the Kingdom at international educational organization meetings and seminars.

The Under-Secretariat for Cultural Affairs and External Relations in the Ministry of Education promotes the cultural, scientific activities in the Kingdom through its patronage of the arts, letters and sciences.

The increased enrollment during the seventies and eighties also witnessed an increase of schools established. In order to administer the schools more efficiently, the Kingdom was divided geographically into school districts. The Ministry of Education sets up the policy and the school districts implement it through superintendents who are appointed by the Ministry. The superintendents exercise general supervision over the operation of the schools within their jurisdiction and are considered the agents of the Ministry who carry out its policies. These school authorities devote most of their time to routine matters related to the day-to-day operation of the schools and are assisted by a number of coordinators (supervisory officers), administrators, and financial officers. While the superintendents are concerned with the total district and work with the Ministry of Education, the school principals are directly responsible for the administration of only one school and have no contact with the Ministry of Education except through the superintendents.

However, in recent years and as part of the administrative reorganization within the Ministry of Education and its components, a great deal of interest has been expressed concerning the need for improving educational administration in the schools. Consequently, efforts were initiated and designed to make schools and school districts more effective. The Ministry of Education began to delegate some of its authority in the management of schools to the local and regional school districts. The reorganization of the school districts indicated an interest in a more decentralized administrative system along with the policy of making the school district superintendent's office an independent unit for the administration of education (Al Salloom, 1974, pp.17-20).

2. **General Presidency of Girls' Education**—The decision by the Saudi government to promote public education for women was resisted by the conservatives and the traditional public, so the government proceeded with caution.

A new organization of less-than-ministerial level was established and entrusted to people of unmistakably traditional views (Manea, 1984). This new organization was the General Presidency of Girls' Education, established in the year 1960 A.D. (1380 A.H.) to be responsible for the girls' education in the same manner as the Ministry of Education is responsible for the boys' education.

The primary responsibilities of the new organization lies in providing general education for female students from kindergarten to secondary and university level. It is also responsible for the training of female teachers.

The founding of the General Presidency of Girls' Education in 1960 marked the beginning of state support for schools and training programs developed specifically for female students. Although some Islamic education has always been available to girls in small religious schools, the Presidency supervised a significant expansion of the educational resources for female students. Elementary education began in 1961 and intermediate and secondary levels followed in 1963. Female students were given the same curricula and were provided with the same type of equipment and physical facilities as the male students.

The General Presidency of Girls' Education supervises the complete spectrum of schooling for female students. The Directorate General for General Education directs schools and programs at the elementary, intermediate and secondary levels. The Deputy General of Girls' Colleges oversees junior college, undergraduate and post-graduate levels. The Presidency devotes some scholarships to female students from Arab and Islamic countries as well as extends monetary and cultural aids. It also administers the specialized training institutes and technical schools such as those devoted to nursing, teacher training, tailoring and adult education.

3. The General Organization for Technical Education and Vocational Training (GOTEVT)

—The lack of trained manpower needed for industrialization made it necessary to implement a strategy that emphasized the increase of educational services as insurance for the country's continual security and welfare after the oil is depleted. Royal Decree No. M. 30 dated 10/8/1400 A.H. (23/6/1980 A.D.) [Ministry of Education, 1988, p.20] established the General Organization for Technical Education and Vocational Training (GOTEVT) to coordinate and implement the Kingdom's manpower development plans and supervise all related training centers and institutes. This organization is headed by a governor who is appointed by royal decree upon the nomination of the Minister of Social Affairs.

GOTEVT evolved from a legacy of technical and vocational education that began in 1949 when the government established the Industrial Preparatory School in Jeddah—the first such specialized institution in the Kingdom. Three divisions of technical education were defined in 1965 when GOTEVT's forerunner, the General Administration for Technical Education, a division of the Ministry of Education, developed separate industrial, trade, and agricultural schools. Initially these technical schools were at the intermediate level, but as general education improved in Saudi Arabia technical schools were supplemented or replaced by secondary level programs.

Vocational training was developed in the mid-1960s under the auspices of the Ministry of Labor and Social Affairs. The Ministry, in collaboration with the International Labor Organization (ILO), established the General Administration of Vocational Training which directed the growing number of vocational centers serving students in every region of the Kingdom. Pre-vocational training centers were developed in 1973 to provide younger trainees with apprentice experience and basic skills.

GOTEVT now has responsibility for both technical education and vocational training, and each of these areas is administered by a Directorate General under the direct authority of the Deputy Governor. While the Directorate General for Technical Education has separate divisions for industrial, commercial, and agricultural education with sections devoted to developing and evaluating examinations and to research and curricula; the Directorate General for Vocational Training has divisions for developing and supervising varied vocational and on-the-job training programs. In addition, separate departments oversee curricula development and program evaluation, trainee affairs, and instructor training and audio-visual aids. All of the Kingdom's provinces now offer technical education and vocational training at three levels: pre-vocational training centers (intermediate level), vocational and commercial secondary schools and higher (post-secondary) technical institutes.

The GOTEVT enjoys financial and administrative independence to perform its role in the development of national vocational and technical manpower, within the framework of the policies set by the "Manpower Council".

4. **The Ministry of Higher Education**—The Ministry of Higher Education was established by Royal Decree No. 236 [Ministry of Education, 1986-88, p.20] dated 8/10/1395 A.H. (1975 A.D.) to implement the Kingdom's higher education policy in the rapidly expanding sphere of post-secondary education. Prior to 1395 A.H. (1975 A.D.), higher education was under the supervision and administration of the Ministry of Education. The Ministry of Higher Education provides support and services for the Kingdom's seven universities and seventy-eight (78) colleges. It is responsible for the supervision, coordination and follow-up of post-secondary programs and the connection with the national development programs in different fields and provides the various sectors with the necessary technical and administrative manpower. It also supervises scholarships of Saudi students studying abroad, coordinates international inter-university relations and oversees the 27 or so educational and cultural mission offices in different countries. The Directorate General for the Development of Higher Education subsumes an assortment of research and development responsibilities which include the collection and analysis of data pertaining to higher education, planning and implementation of education policy and programs, research and translation of relevant scholarship, and coordination of educational policy requirements with other government departments. Within the purview of the Ministry are special research institutes such as the World Advocacy for Muslim Youth and specialized scholarship programs for government officials.

The University Council in each university is headed by the Minister of Higher Education, except for the Islamic University whose council is headed by the Custodian of the Two Holy Mosques, King Fahd Ibn Abdulaziz.

Of the four government agencies devoted to education in Saudi Arabia, the Ministry of Education is by far the largest and most complex since it is a policy-making body in addition to being an administrative bureau. The other three agencies--the Ministry of Higher Education, General Presidency of Girls' Education and the General Organization for Technical Education and Vocational Training—specialize in the development and administration of their respective segments of the educational system. National policy ensures that the efforts of these separate agencies are integrated in successful collaboration toward the common goal of improving the educational resources available to Saudi citizens.

5) **Others**—In addition to these four government agencies, there are some other authorities who are active participants in the fields of general, technical, and girls' education. Some of these are the following: the Ministry of Defense which provides general education for its personnel and their families; the National Guard, likewise provides similar services; the Ministry of Interior which established new elementary, intermediate and adult education classes; the Ministry of Social Affairs which established social guidance institutions for children in the elementary and intermediate education levels, as well as supervises other vocational and technical programs offered by the private sector (Ministry of Education, 1988, p. 13) and the Ministry of Health which established some health institutes and nursing schools.

In the field of higher education, in addition to the Staff Military Academy, the Ministry of Defense and Aviation established three military academies responsible for the preparation of the necessary cadres in the areas of land, sea, and air defense.

King Khaled Military College is an institution of higher learning with the main mission of training officers for the National Guard. It was established in December, 1982 with a three-year college program that leads to a Bachelor of Military Science degree. Subjects are balanced between academic and military.

The Ministry of Interior has King Fahd Security College which trains students in security matters. Also the Ministry has two specialized institutes, one for traffic and the other for immigration and passport administration.

In addition, there are four civil aviation junior college level training institutes which follow the Presidency of Civil Aviation.

V. DESCRIPTION OF LEVELS OF EDUCATION IN SAUDI ARABIA

This chapter describes the different levels of education in the Kingdom of Saudi Arabia. The following Flow Chart of Education in the Kingdom, 1990/91, (refer to Table 2) provides a better perspective and understanding of the education system. The objectives specified for these educational levels in the national education policy are also described fully and include data on student enrollment, schools, teachers, teacher qualifications and curricula.

Education in Saudi Arabia is divided into five levels: pre-first level, Kindergarten; first level, Elementary; second level, Intermediate; third level, Secondary Education; and fourth level, Higher Education. The number of years for the first four levels are as follows: pre-first level, Kindergarten—2 years; first level, Elementary—6 years; second level, Intermediate Education—3 years; third level, Secondary Education—3 years. Upon completion of the second level of Intermediate education a student makes an early career decision or is advised on his career path. He proceeds either to 3 years of regular Secondary Education or to 3 years of Technical Secondary Education (grades 1-3). Students who choose the Regular Secondary Education proceed to the fourth level of Higher Education, and they choose one of the following programs: a 4-year bachelor's degree in teaching from the Teachers' Colleges; a 4-year bachelor's degree in a field other than engineering or medicine; or 1-year preparatory program for those in the engineering and medical fields plus 4 years in Engineering or Medicine proper which can lead to postgraduate levels of master's and doctorate degrees. Upon completion of the 3 years of Technical Secondary Education, those who choose a career path in vocational or technical field take a 2-year higher education program in the intermediate colleges allowing more specialization in the fields of technical commercial and technical industrial education. Those in the technical industrial field can become teachers upon completion of a 1-year program in the Higher Institute for Teachers' Education.

TABLE 2
FLOW CHART OF EDUCATION IN THE KINGDOM OF SAUDI ARABIA 1990/91

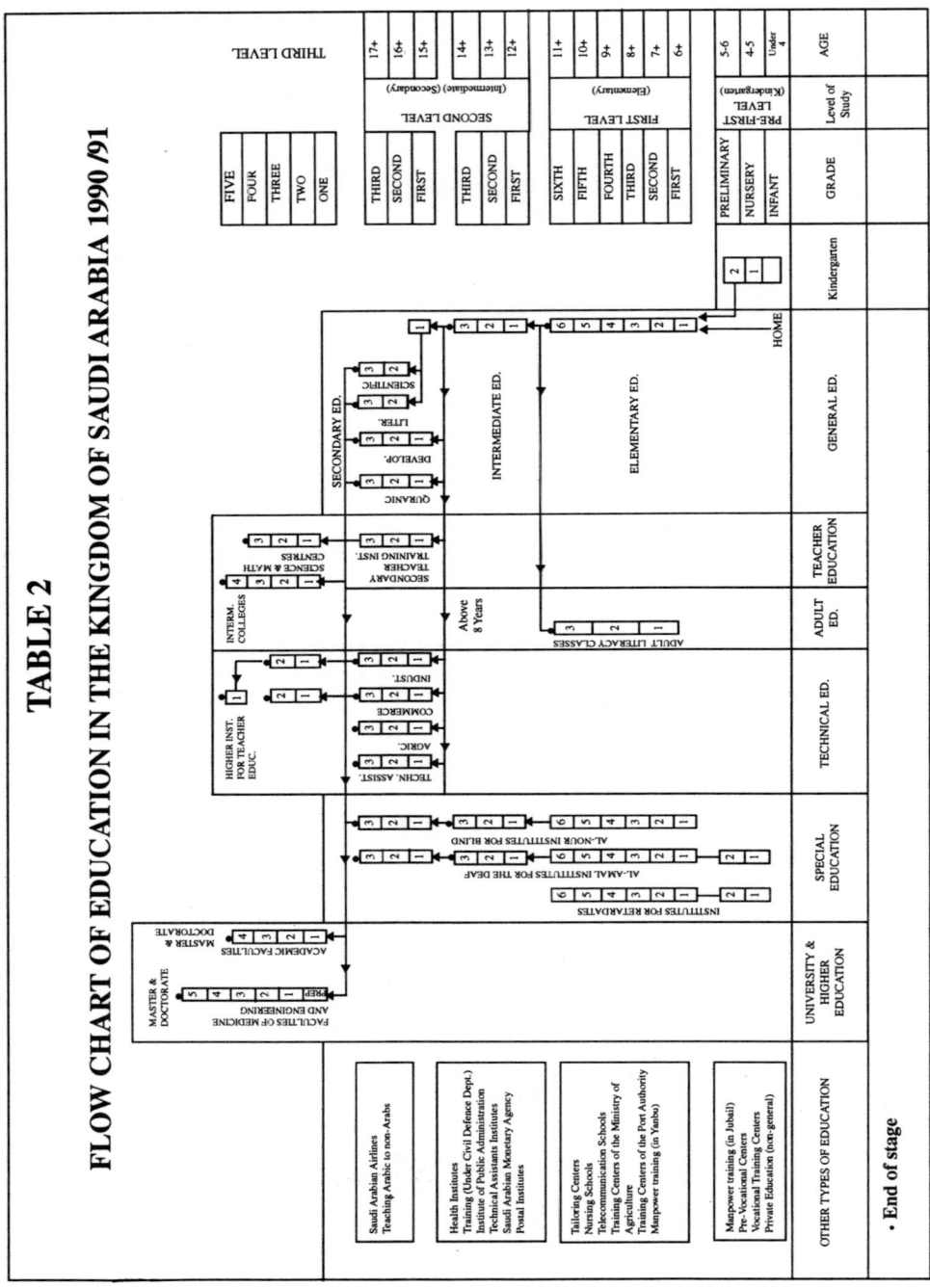

- End of stage

1. PRE-FIRST LEVEL—Kindergarten

The first level of education in the Kingdom starts with kindergarten. Although optional, Saudi educational policy supports kindergarten programs as part of the concerted effort to raise overall educational standards in the country. Kindergarten provides a constructive educational environment for very young children in which basic social behavior and hygiene are emphasized, along with an array of play activities. Most pre-kindergarten and kindergarten schools in Saudi Arabia are coeducational and are under the direct supervision of the General Presidency of Girls' Education which supervises their programs and curricula, whether public or private, except for 1 which is under the Ministry of Education.

Kindergarten is classified into different age groups, namely: infant groups for children under four (4) years of age, nursery for four to five year-olds, and preliminary groups for five to six year-olds. There are also some special kindergarten programs for gifted children at the preliminary level.

A day in kindergarten school starts from 8:00 in the morning until 1:00 in the afternoon and the curriculum includes the following daily activities:

8:00- 8:30	Play, recreation
8:30- 9:00	Breakfast
9:00- 9:45	Garden, playing with pets
9:45-10:45	Oral composition, reading, writing
10:45-11:15	Singing, chanting
11:45-12:15	Lunch, followed by health education
12:15- 1:00	Stories, library, creative play or religious education

Kindergarten, being the earliest stage of education, is characterized by the tender treatment and general orientation of children. Government educational policy states the following objectives for kindergarten programs: Kindergarten education should:

1. nurture the instincts of children and look after their moral, mental and physical growth in a natural environment similar to that provided by their family and which complies with the requirements of Islam;
2. shape the child's religious inclination according to the Islamic belief in the unity of God;
3. teach children good conduct and help them to acquire the virtues of Islam by giving them a positive example at school;
4. familiarize children with the school atmosphere and assist their socialization into school life;
5. teach children fundamental knowledge and skills that are related to

their surroundings and that are suitable to their age group;
6. teach children proper personal hygiene and enhance their creativity and aesthetic sense;
7. encourage children's imaginative thinking and guide their development;
8. care for children's needs and happiness without spoiling or burdening them;
9. protect children against danger, treat early signs of bad conduct and confront childhood problems.

Table 3 below shows the total number of schools, students, teachers and classes for the kindergarten level for the years 1404 A.H./1984 A.D. and 1414 A.H./1994 A.D. respectively.

The number of kindergarten schools increased by ninety-nine percent over a 11-year period, from 377 schools in 1404 A.H./1984 A.D. to 749 schools in 1414 A.H./1994 A.D.

The number of kindergarten teachers, most of whom had qualifications either from secondary or junior college level teacher training programs, increased by approximately one hundred fifty-eight percent over this same 11-year period, from 2,298 teachers in 1404 A.H./1984 A.D. to 5,926 teachers in 1414 A.H./1994 A.D. An eighty percent increase in the kindergarten student enrollment, from 47,197 students to 85,367 students, lowered the student-teacher ratio from approximately 20:1 in 1404 A.H./1984 A.D. to approximately 14:1 in 1414 A.H./1994 A.D.

TABLE 3
Total Number of Schools, Students, Teachers, and Classes at the Kindergarten level, for School Years 1404 & 1414 A.H.

	Schools		Students		Teachers		Classes	
Supervising Agency	1404	1414	1404	1414	1404	1414	1404	1414
Ministry of Education	1	1	939	472	50	52	40	18
Pres. of Girls' Educ.	123	206	7041	16929	551	1795	359	949
Gov't Agencies	—	199	—	24201	—	1344	—	1151
Private	253	343	39217	43765	1697	2735	1475	2266
TOTAL	377	749	47197	85367	2298	5926	1874	4384

Sources:
1. Ministry of Finance and National Economy, 1404 A.H.
2. Ministry of Education, and General Presidency of Girls' Education, 1412-1413.

2. FIRST LEVEL—ELEMENTARY EDUCATION

The next level of education is the Elementary level which is considered as the crux of the government's educational expansion program and perceived as a major force in the integration of isolated segments of the traditionally oriented population into the society. Only the Elementary level schooling is compulsory in Saudi Arabia. It is also regarded as the foundation for the development of an overall education program.

Elementary education spans grades 1-6, after an optional completion of one or two years of kindergarten. It provides learning emphasis on classical Arabic language and the Islamic religion with secondary stress on history, geography, mathematics and in some cases, English (refer to Table 4). Children begin elementary school at six years of age and students in each grade are generally within a two year age span.

GRADE	AGES OF STUDENTS
1	6- 8
2	7- 9
3	8-10
4	9-11
5	10-12
6	11-14

The school year consists of two semesters, each with fourteen weeks of classes and a two-week examination period. The elementary school schedule has six daily class periods which are each forty-five minutes long. The standard curriculum shown below is studied by the boys and girls in their separate schools.

The Saudi school system, at all levels of general education, is built on a series of yearly promotion examinations which all students must pass in order to advance to the next grade. Elementary level examinations were nationally standardized until 1981 when it became the responsibility of individual schools to prepare and administer examinations to their students. Students must pass the examinations in all subjects. A student may be retested for failure in any subject before the end of the summer. However, failing the retest results in the student repeating the grade level for another year. Promotion to the intermediate level requires the earning of the Elementary School Certificate through passing a standard examination. The success rate on this examination has been consistently high through the last decade, averaging about a ninety percent passing rate.

Saudi educational policy states that elementary education should: (Educ. Policy, pp. 16-17)

1. Lay the foundation for all later stages in life and provide all members of Saudi society with the fundamentals of sound ideology, learning experience, knowledge and skills;

2. Cultivate the correct Islamic creed in children's souls and provide them with a comprehensive moral and intellectual education shaped by Islamic values;

3. Teach students Islamic prayers, virtues and good conduct;

4. Develop children's basic skills, especially in language, mathematics and physical education;

5. Further children's general education in all subjects;

6. Acquaint children with the blessings God has bestowed on them and the geographical and social environment of their nation so they can utilize these blessings in service to their community;

7. Develop children's aesthetic sense and imaginative thinking, and strengthen their appreciation of manual and technical work of all kinds;

8. Develop children's understanding of the rights and duties of citizenship and instill love of country and loyalty to the monarchy;

9. Cultivate a love for learning and the value of work, and train children to make constructive use of their leisure time;

10. Prepare children for future responsibilities as part of Saudi society.

Significant progress has been made in elementary education over the past years. Unprecedented growth in the number of boy's elementary schools in the 1970s was attributed to the impetus provided by the Kingdom's First Five-Year Development Plan 1970-1975 which registered 1,500 public elementary schools between the period 1960 and 1975 (Natto and Khan, 1976). The achievements of the first plan far exceeded the targets set by the government for elementary education. The percentage of Saudi children attending school at all levels is rising steadily. It is the elementary level, however, that has grown most dramatically. Table 5-A below indicates that a total of 2,148,998 students, both boys and girls, enrolled in 1414 A.H./1994 A.D., an increase of approximately eighty-four percent, from the 1,166,604 students enrolled in 1404 A.H./1984 A.D. Table 5-B below shows that the rate of increase in the male student population, which registered at approximately sixty percent, from 676,281 students in 1404 A.H./1984 A.D. to 1,085,242 students in 1414 A.H./1994 A.D. was lower than that of the one hundred seventeen percent increase in the female student population, which registered at 490,323 in 1404 A.H. and 1,063,756 in 1414 A.H., respectively. In 1414 A.H., the male students accounted for fifty-one percent or 1,085,242 and the female students, forty-nine percent or 1,063,756, of the total elementary student population. The total number of elementary schools increased by fifty percent, from 7,259 schools in 1404 A.H./1984 A.D. to 10,890 schools ten years later. It also shows that, of this increase in 1414 A.H./1994 A.D., the boys' schools accounted for 52% or 5,632 and the girls' schools accounted for 48% or 5,258, of the total number of elementary schools.

TABLE 4
ELEMENTARY SCHOOL CURRICULUM
Subject and Hours per Week

SUBJECTS	GRADES					
	First	Second	Third	Fourth	Fifth	Sixth
Islamic Studies	9	9	9	9	9	9
Arabic Studies	9	9	9	8	8	8
Social Studies	0	0	0	2	2	2
Science	2	2	2	2	3	3
Mathematics	4	4	4	5	5	5
Art Education	2	2	2	1	1	1
Physical Education (Boys Only)	2	2	2	2	2	2
Home Economics (Girls Only)	0	0	0	2	2	2
Total Hours (Boys)	28	28	28	29	30	30
Per Week (Girls)	26	26	26	29	30	30

Source: *Ministry of Education,* 1978, pp. 16-17

As shown in Table 5-C, the one hundred and three percent increase in the number of elementary level teachers, from 73,057 in 1404 A.H./1984 A.D. to 148,082 in 1414 A.H./1994 A.D., decreased the student-teacher ratio from approximately 16:1 in 1404 A.H./1984 A.D. to approximately 14:1 in 1414 A.H./1994 A.D. Also there was a 132% increase in the number of Saudi elementary teachers over this 11-year period. Despite the 7,992 figure of combined Saudi and Non-Saudi teachers in 1414 A.H./1994 A.D., the number of Saudi teachers still accounted for 74% of the entire teacher population.

TABLE 5-A
Total Number of Schools, Students, Teachers, and Classes at the Elementary level, by Supervising Agency, for School Years 1404 & 1414 A.H.

SUPERVISING AGENCY	SCHOOLS 1404	SCHOOLS 1414	STUDENTS 1404	STUDENTS 1414	TEACHERS 1404	TEACHERS 1414	CLASSES 1404	CLASSES 1414
Ministry of Education	4323	5417	646694	1015401	42783	68200	33191	50194
Pres. of Girls' Educ.	2754	4528	466353	909024	27414	61202	21170	41242
Other Gov't Agencies	42	433	11178	110381	554	7934	399	4392
Private	140	512	42379	114192	2306	10746	1612	5855
TOTAL	7259	10890	1166604	2148998	73057	148082	56372	101683

Sources:
1. Ministry of Finance and National Economy, 1404 A.H.
2. Ministry of Education and General Presidency of Girls's Education Statistical Charts for School Year 1414 A.H

TABLE 5-B
Total Number of Schools, Students, and Classes at the Elementary level, by Boys and/or Girls, for School Years 1404 & 1414 A.H.

GENDER	SCHOOLS 1404	SCHOOLS 1414	STUDENTS 1404	STUDENTS 1414	CLASSES 1404	CLASSES 1414
Boys	4423	5632	676281	1085242	34269	53535
Girls	2836	5258	490323	1063756	22103	48148
TOTAL	7259	10890	1166604	2148998	56372	101683

Sources:
1. Ministry of Finance and National Economy, 1404 A.H.
2. Ministry of Education and General Presidency of Girls's Education Statistical Charts for School Year 1414 A.H.

TABLE 5-C
Total Number of Teachers at the Elementary level, by Saudi and Non-Saudi, for School Years 1404 & 1414 A.H.

NATIONALITY	1404	1414
Saudi	47551	110137
Non-Saudi	25506	29953
Nationality Unspecified	—*	7992
TOTAL	73057	148082

*No available data.

Sources:
1. Ministry of Finance and National Economy, 1404 A.H.
2. Ministry of Education and General Presidency of Girls's Education Statistical Charts for School Year 1414 A.H.

The majority of these teachers had qualifications from teacher training programs at the secondary and junior college levels. Some had qualifications including higher degrees such as a bachelor's, master's or doctorate degree. Recent changes, however, in teacher qualification standards require all new teachers to complete bachelor's degrees and for teachers who have training certificates to be upgraded. Teacher training programs are also trying to redress the shortage of male teachers and native Saudi teachers. The number of Saudi teachers at all levels has been growing steadily.

The private schools, which account for only four percent of the elementary schools in the Kingdom, employ the same government-developed curricula and examination system used in the public schools. This is also the case for all the small number of government-supported elementary schools supervised by other government agencies such as the Ministry of Defense, Ministry of Social Affairs, the Islamic University and Imam Mohammad Ibn Saud Islamic University. These schools are required to meet all the standards established by the Ministry of Education for regular public schools. Most private schools are administered by a headmaster who is a government employee appointed by the Ministry of Education to ensure compliance with government regulation and to administer benefits given by the government to private schools.

3. SECOND LEVEL—INTERMEDIATE

Upon finishing the elementary level, students between the ages twelve and fifteen are encouraged to continue on to the intermediate level which consists of three years, the equivalent of grades 7-9 in the U.S. education system. The intermediate level furthers students' general education and the study of Islamic culture. In the preceding elementary level students with practical and applied inclinations are guided toward the intermediate level with vocational technology in mind.

The objectives for intermediate education outlined in state policy are to: (Ministry of Educ., pp. 17-18)

1. Give children a comprehensive Islamic education to enrich body, mind and soul;

2. Teach students the skills and knowledge that suit their age and stage of development;

3. Stimulate students to seek knowledge through meditation and scientific reasoning;

4. Develop, orient and refine students' intellectual skills;

5. Instill respect for the social life of Islam which is marked by fraternity, cooperation, sense of duty and responsibility;

6. Train students to serve their communities and country, and strengthen their loyalty to the monarchy;

7. Stimulate students to restore the glory of the Islamic nation and march on the path of dignity and glory;

8. Train students to devote their time to useful reading, invest their leisure time in constructive activities, and work toward strengthening and advancing their Islamic character;

9. Enable students to be aware of and confront misleading propaganda, subversive doctrines and principles foreign to Islamic values;

10. Prepare students for the next stage of life.

TABLE 6
INTERMEDIATE SCHOOL CURRICULUM
Subject and Hours per Week

SUBJECTS	GRADES		
	First	Second	Third
Islamic Studies	8	8	8
Arabic Studies	6	6	6
English	4	4	4
Science	4	4	4
Mathematics	4	4	4
Art Education	2	2	2
Physical Education (Boys Only)	1	1	1
Home Economics (Girls Only)	1	1	1
TOTAL HOURS (BOYS)	29	29	29
PER WEEK (GIRLS)	29	29	29

Source: *Ministry of Education*, 1978, pp 17-18.

The school year at this level consists of two semesters that are fifteen weeks long, plus a two-week examination period. There are thirty-three class periods per week, each forty-five minutes in length. The intermediate school curriculum includes the subjects listed in Table 6.

English becomes a required subject and remains compulsory throughout secondary school. Passing a completion examination is necessary to receive the Intermediate School Certificate, which is a pre-requisite for continuting on to secondary school.

Tables 7-A & 7-B show that in 1404 A.H./1984 A.D. there were 2,098 intermediate schools, of which 1,388 were for boys with an enrollment of 212,042 and 710 were for girls with an enrollment of 123,317. These increased to 4,493 in 1414 A.H./1994 A.D., of which 2,471 were for boys with an enrollment of 380,877 and 2,022 were for girls with an enrollment of 336,656.

Public intermediate schools in 1414 A.H./1994 A.D., numbering 4,257, accounted for approximately 95% of the educational institutions at this level. The remaining 5% consisted of 236 private schools.

Majority of the intermediate school teachers had bachelor's degrees and others had qualifications from Intermediate, Secondary or Junior college level teacher training programs. Master's degrees were held by a small percentage of intermediate level teachers. The new standard requires a bachelor's degree for all new teachers and comparable upgrading of qualifications for those with less training. This applies to teachers of all levels including the Intermediate level.

Table 7-C shows a remarkable 313% increase in the number of Saudi teachers in comparison to a 19% increase of non-Saudi teachers at the intermediate level over an eleven-year period. Of the total 57,949 intermediate level teachers, 64% or 37,093 were Saudis and 32% or 18,244 non-Saudis.

Upon completion of the 3-year intermediate level, a student may proceed to choose from the following three options: a) regular secondary education which leads to further higher education of Bachelor's, Master's and Doctoral degrees; b) vocational and technical education that leads to further training in the Higher Institute for Teacher Education for those who aspire to become teachers in the field of vocational and technical education; c) a career in education through teacher training colleges which may also lead to higher education. Following are descriptions of each of these choices:

TABLE 7-A
Total Number of Schools, Students, Teachers, and Classes at the Intermediate level, by Supervising Agency, for School years 1404 & 1414 A.H.

	SCHOOLS		STUDENTS		TEACHERS		CLASSES	
SUPERVISING AGENCY	1404	1414	1404	1414	1404	1414	1404	1414
Ministry of Education	1219	2349	180666	336162	13579	28401	6972	14980
Pres. of Girls' Educ.	679	1680	119064	321137	8921	24121	4560	11431
Other Gov't Agencies	124	228	24340	39861	1206	3066	757	1560
Private	76	236	11289	20373	601	2361	413	1278
T O T A L	2098	4493	335359	717533	24307	57949	12702	29249

Sources:
1. Ministry of Finance and National Economy, 1404 A.H.
2. Ministry of Education and General Presidency of Girls' Education Statistical Charts for School Year 1414 A.H.

TABLE 7-B
Total Number of Schools, Students, and Classes at the Intermediate level, by Boys and/or Girls, for School years 1404 & 1414 A.H.

GENDER	SCHOOLS		STUDENTS		CLASSES	
	1404	1414	1404	1414	1404	1414
Boys	1388	2471	212042	380877	7977	15813
Girls	710	2022	123317	336656	4725	13436
TOTAL	2098	4493	335359	717533	12702	29249

Sources:
1. Ministry of Finance and National Economy, 1404 A.H.
2. Ministry of Education and General Presidency of Girls' Education Statistical Charts for School Year 1414 A.H. .

TABLE 7-C
Total Number of Teachers at the Intermediate level, by Saudi and Non-Saudi, for School years 1404 & 1414 A.H.

NATIONALITY	1404	1414
Saudi	8974	37093
Non-Saudi	15333	18244
Nationality Unspecified	—*	2612
TOTAL	24307	57949

*No available data.

Sources:
1. Ministry of Finance and National Economy, 1404 A.H.
2. Ministry of Education and General Presidency of Girls's Education Statistical Charts for School Year 1414 A.H.

4) THIRD LEVEL— SECONDARY EDUCATION

The brief history of secondary education in Saudi Arabia started with the opening of the first secondary school in 1926 with a curriculum consisting mainly of religious and Arabic studies. Later, English, Mathematics, and the Natural Sciences were introduced. By the end of the World War II, the entire country was served by only seven (7) secondary schools, all located in the western province of Al Hijaz (Salloom, 1974). According to this study, "Secondary education was based on the European system and consisted of a five-year course." In 1958, it became a three-year program, which was separate from intermediate or junior high school. By 1970, the Ministry of Education operated 24 schools with a student population of 8,242 (Gohaidan, 1981). The secondary education's objectives are: 1) religious orientation; 2) development of scientific attitude and academic practices; 3) preparation for Higher Education; and 4) the preparation of the non-college bound students. The following outline describes the policy concerning secondary education: (Min. of Educ., pp. 19-21)

1. Strengthening all aspects of Islamic faith and compliance with Islamic principles in all deeds.

2. Strengthening students' knowledge of Islamic doctrine and instilling pride in Islam so that they can preach and defend their faith.

3. Confirming students' membership in the Islamic nation and belief in the one God.

4. Instilling allegiance to the wide Islamic homeland and private homeland (the Kingdom of Saudi Arabia).

5. Directing students' talents and skills into the most fruitful paths to serve their personal goals and the objectives of Islamic education.

6. Developing students' scientific thinking and the spirit of research, systematic analysis, and sound academic methods.

7. Opening opportunities to capable students and enabling them to continue their studies in all levels and specialties of higher education.

8. Preparing students not destined for further academic study for fulfilling and appropriate work.

9. Graduating technically and morally qualified students to fill the country's needs in elementary teaching, religious duties and occupations in farming, trade, and industry.

10. Establishing the importance of family solidarity as the foundation for a solid, Islamic family unit.

11. Providing students with guidance through the emotional turmoil and development of the teenage years.

12. Instilling students with the virtues of useful reading, the desire for

knowledge, the value of fruitful work, and the importance of using their leisure time to benefit their personal goals and community conditions.

13. Enhancing students' consciousness so they can confront subversive or misleading ideas.

Over the last several years two types of secondary education programs developed in Saudi Arabia -- the Regular Secondary program and the experimental Modern Secondary program that allowed students greater flexibility in the shaping of their education. The trial period for the Modern Secondary curriculum ended in the fall of 1990 and a decision was made to phase it out by 1993. Both programs are described below.

a) REGULAR SECONDARY

Secondary school education spans three years and generally serves students in the fifteen to nineteen year-old age group. All students in the regular secondary schools study a general curriculum for the first year and choose a liberal arts or science emphasis for the remaining two years. Students who maintain high grade point averages in mathematics and physical sciences at the 10th grade level are encouraged to enroll in the science program, while those with low grade point averages are normally assigned to the literary concentration. The curriculum includes the courses listed in the chart below.

The school year consists of two semesters, each of which is twenty weeks long, including a two week examination period. Class periods are forty-five minutes long and weekly schedules vary between a total of twenty-six and thirty-three periods, depending on grade and subject emphasis. To earn a Secondary School Certificate students must complete the required credits and pass their individual subject examinations with a grade no less than fifty percent of the maximum score.

b) MODERN SECONDARY

The Modern Secondary program, phased out in 1993, offered broad choices of subjects and courses that permitted students to tailor programs that suit their future goals. The system encouraged students to take more responsibility and play an active role in shaping their education. After the first semester, students had a choice to pursue a science curriculum (Chemistry, Physics and Mathematics) or a literary curriculum (general studies, commercial and religious studies). Students were able to change divisions at the beginning of subsequent semesters and transfer all their course credits. A total of 168 semester hours was required to graduate; 67 hours of general program core courses, 78 hours of division and department major courses, and 23 hours of electives. Additional graduation requirements included a minimum average of "Pass" in all courses and subject exams. Upon graduation students received a Modern Secondary Certificate.

The phase out of the Modern Secondary program consequently discountinued the use of the credit hour system at the secondary level throughout the Kingdom, effective from the first grade secondary level, school year 1991/92. The following directives were issued by the Ministry of Education for adaptation of this change in policy:

1. The gradual phase out of the Modern Secondary program and its use of the credit hour system started with the first grade level in 1992/93 (1412) followed by the second grade level in 1993/94 (1413) and finally the third grade level by 1994/95 (1414). Students who graduated from the intermediate school in 1411 were accepted into the first grade level of the Regular Secondary program of 1992/93 (1412).

2. Students admitted to the secondary school on or before 1991 (1411) who wish to continue in the Modern Secondary Program may do so provided they graduate by 1994/95 (1414). Those who do not or cannot graduate by 1994/95 (1414) shall have their credits evaluated according to the following:

    a) Students can be promoted to the second grade level either in the science or literature major if they successfully complete 56 credit hours, of which 50 credit hours are subjects from the general curriculum;

    b) Students can be promoted to the third grade level if they successfully complete 112 credit hours, of which 50 credit hours are subjects from the general curriculum and 40 credit hours are subjects from their major;

    c) Students can be promoted to the third grade level in the social science major if they successfully complete 112 credit hours, of which 50 credit hours are subjects from the general curriculum and 40 credit hours are subjects from either Islamic & Arabic study or administration & humanities studies.

3. Students can transfer from the Modern Secondary system back to the Regular Secondary system, according to the above-mentioned evaluation criteria;

4. The decision to transfer students from the Modern system to the Regular Secondary system depends on the Regional Education Authority subject to the availability of facilities, manpower, and number of students desiring to transfer;

5. Students who wish to transfer from the Modern system to the Regular Secondary system at the second grade level, but cannot meet the requirements to do so shall remain in the first grade level of the secondary program. This also applies to those who wish to go to the third grade level;

6. Students who successfully meet the requirements to transfer to the second and third grade level, major in science or social science of the Regular Secondary program, which does not use the credit hour system, are provided with textbooks in these two fields.

Secondary religious institutes, run by Imam Mohammed bin Saud Islamic University and the Islamic University, offer an alternative to male students who wish to emphasize Islamic and Arabic studies. These Qur'anic Secondary schools replaced the science requirements found in the Regular Secondary curriculum (refer to Table 8) with religious subjects. Graduates receive a Religious Institute Secondary School Certificate. As shown in Tables 9-A & 9-B, there was an increase of 1,157 schools at the secondary level in the ten-year period, from 803 schools in 1404 A.H./1984 A.D. to 1,960 schools in 1414 A.H./1994 A.D., which was a 122% increase. Of this, the secondary schools for boys accounted for 53%, while the secondary schools for girls accounted for 47%. A sharp increase of 605 secondary schools for girls occurred during this time, from 270 schools in 1404 A.H./1984 A.D. to 875 schools in 1414 A.H./1994 A.D., equivalent to a 213% increase.

As shown in Table 9-A, student enrollment totalled 378,441 in 1414 A.H./1994 A.D., which is an increase of approximately 157% from the 1404 A.H./1984 A.D. figure of 146,981. It is interesting to note that the rate of increase in female student enrollment increased by 216%, exceeding that of the rate of increase in male student enrollment which registered at a lower 118%. In terms of number, however, the male student population accounted for 51% of the entire secondary level's student population and the female student population accounted for the remaining 49%. The student-teacher ratio decreased slightly at this level, from 15:1 in 1404 A.H./1984 A.D. to 14:1 in 1414 A.H./1994 A.D. Of the 27,150 teachers reported in 1414 A.H./1994 A.D. at the secondary level, over 90 percent had bachelor's degrees (Ministry of Education, 1991/92).

TABLE 8
REGULAR SECONDARY CURRICULUM
Subjects and Hours Per Week

Subject Areas	Grades Courses	General Program	Humanities Section		Science Section	
		1	2	3	2	3
Islamic Studies	Holy Qur'an-Recitation	1	1	1	1	1
	Hadith	1	1	1	1	1
	Towhd	1	1	1	1	1
	Fiqh	1	1	0	1	0
	T O T A L	4	4	3	4	3
Arabic Studies	Grammar	3	3	3	2	2
	Rhetoric	1	2	2	0	0
	Literature	3	3	3	1	1
	Composition	1	1	1	1	0
	Reading	1	2	2	0	0
	T O T A L	9	11	11	4	3
Social Studies	History	2	3	2	0	0
	Geography	2	2	3	0	0
	Psychology	0	2	0	0	0
	Sociology	0	0	2	0	0
	T O T A L	4	7	7	0	0
Sciences	Physics	2	0	0	4	4
	Chemistry	2	0	0	4	4
	Biology	2	0	0	3	3
	Geology	0	0	0	1	1
	T O T A L	6	0	0	12	12
Mathematics		5	0	0	7	7
English		4	4	4	4	4
Physical Education (Boys Only)		1	1	1	1	1
Home Economics (Girls Only)		1	1	1	1	1
TOTAL HOURS PER WEEK	Boys and Girls	33	27	26	32	30

TABLE 9-A
Total Number of Schools, Students, Teachers, and Classes at the Secondary level, by Supervising Agency, for School Years 1404 & 1414 A.H.

SUPERVISING AGENCY	SCHOOLS		STUDENTS		TEACHERS		CLASSES	
	1404	1414	1404	1414	1404	1414	1404	1414
Ministry of Education	418	849	72304	175147	4608	11400	2832	6393
Pres. of Girls' Educ.	250	797	56542	165329	4295	13578	2098	6225
Other Gov't Agencies	82	177	13389	20530	691	760	454	970
Private	53	137	4746	17435	358	1412	231	834
TOTAL	803	1960	146981	378441	9952	27150	5615	14422

Sources:
1. Ministry of Finance and National Economy, 1404 A.H.
2. Ministry of Education and General Presidency of Girls' Education Statistical Charts for School Year 1414 A.H.

TABLE 9-B
Total Number of Schools, Students, and Classes at the Secondary level, by Boys and/or Girls, for School Years 1404 & 1414 A.H.

GENDER	SCHOOLS		STUDENTS		CLASSES	
	1404	1414	1404	1414	1404	1414
Boys	533	1085	88209	192694	3400	7257
Girls	270	875	58772	185747	2215	7165
TOTAL	803	1960	146981	378441	5615	14422

Sources:
1. Ministry of Finance and National Economy, 1404 A.H.
2. Ministry of Education and General Presidency of Girls' Education Statistical Charts for School Year 1414 A.H.

TABLE 9-C
Total Number of Teachers at the Secondary level, by Saudi and/or Non-Saudi, for School Years 1404 & 1414 A.H.

NATIONALITY	1404	1414
Saudi	2736	17039
Non-Saudi	7216	9619
Nationality Unspecified	—	492
TOTAL	9952	27150

Sources:
1. Ministry of Finance and National Economy, 1404 A.H.
2. Ministry of Education and General Presidency of Girls' Education Statistical Charts for School Year 1414 A.H.

c) VOCATIONAL AND TECHNICAL SECONDARY

National development policy makes a compelling case for the importance of technical education and vocational training in Saudi Arabia. Current policy aims to protect Islamic values and upgrade the living standards of Saudi citizens while maintaining social and economic stability. This is to be achieved by increasing the growth of the gross national product, diversifying national income resources, concentrating on industrial production and developing human resources so that all sectors of society can participate fully in this process. Upgrading the technical and vocational skills of the Saudi work force is a critical factor in increasing productivity and staying apace with the rapid technological developments sweeping the international business world. The programs in industrial, commercial, agricultural, and vocational training described here play an essential role in preparing more highly skilled Saudi workers.

In 1980, Royal Decree No. M130 was issued to establish an organization to take full responsibility for vocational and technical education and training in the country. The General Organization for Technical Education and Vocational Training (GOTEVT) was formed in response to those who called for one organization that would consolidate and centralize the administration in order to develop the training programs that were scattered among several government agencies. In order to fulfill the Kingdom's manpower requirements, GOTEVT established the following objectives:

1. To prepare individuals to work in industrial, commercial and agricultural fields, and help to develop the national economy through

providing a competent technical work force that can enter the public or private sectors or government ministries;

2. To provide individuals with an Islamic foundation for high moral standards, strong faith, and ability to reason and adapt to changing circumstances;

3. To offer a broad scientific base for technical manpower in order to optimize an individual worker's response to rapid technological change;

4. To allow individuals the opportunity to learn a trade and continue their training to the highest level suited to their mental and physical abilities;

5. To develop technicians' skills and continuously upgrade their vocational knowledge;

6. To emphasize the dignity of manual and vocational work and the important role they play in national development;

7. To discourage internal migration to big cities by spreading vocational training centers throughout all regions of the Kingdom.

GOTEVT's strategy for implementing these objectives is based on education, research and planning. National policy holds that providing a full range of educational opportunities in technical and vocational fields is an indispensable means of preparing a capable work force. Furthermore, by providing special morning and evening training courses, those individuals working as unskilled laborers or those unable to continue academic study can be trained to work in new fields.

Research focused on technical manpower problems and shifting labor market requirements is used to design and evaluate the educational framework, an ongoing process that seeks to integrate theory and practice. An aggressive program of incentives, including trainee benefits, credit toward work experience, automatic entry into or upgrading within the civil service, and business loans for graduates helps to enhance the accessibility and appeal of technical education and vocational training for the Saudi work force.

GOTEVT supervises three levels of vocational and technical education: the secondary, junior college (intermediate technical colleges) and college (higher technical institute) levels.

Trainees enrolled in all secondary level technical education and vocational training programs receive standard benefits from the government such as: a monthly stipend, free work clothes, educational materials, lodging, meals and daily transportation to and from school. Secondary institute graduates are also eligible for government loans to start a private business and the best qualified graduates can continue their training at a college of technology. Graduates who work as instructors in vocational training centers receive a 20 percent increase in their stipends as teaching allowance which increases further to 30 percent after five years. Graduates can also pursue further studies at the intermediate technical colleges and at the higher technical institute in order to qualify for teaching positions in a secondary industrial institute.

There are standard admission requirements for all secondary level technical educational and vocational training programs. These requirements are: 1) a Good Behavior Certificate from the last school attended; 2) passing of a medical examination which should indicate non-existence of major disabilities; 3) Saudi citizenship; and 4) an Intermediate School Certificate. Below are tables that show what has been achieved in the technical and vocational education in terms of the number of schools, students, teachers and classes. Technical education is divided into industrial, commercial, agricultural while vocational training includes dressmaking/tailoring, cooking, and others. A brief summary of each of these sections is also provided below.

TECHNICAL INDUSTRIAL EDUCATION

In the eleven-year period from 1404 A.H./1984 A.D. to 1414 A.H./1994 A.D., the number of secondary industrial schools remained constant at 8 as shown in Table 10-A. Student enrollment increased, however, from 3,698 in 1404 A.H./1984 A.D. to 8,672 in 1414 A.H./1994 A.D. The number of teachers likewise increased by 481 in number, from 645 in 1404 A.H./1984 A.D. to 1,126 in 1414 A.H./1994 A.D., or approximately 75% increase. Of the 1,126 teachers, 632 or 56% were Saudi and the remaining 494 or 44% were Non-Saudi teachers. These institutes have three-year programs for the Intermediate School graduates in which training is offered in four areas:

1. Mechanical Department:
a) General Mechanics—training in lathes, scraping, drilling and grinding machines, and hydraulic and pneumatic equipment;

b) Metal Work—training in welding, blacksmithing, and metal furniture manufacturing;

c) Agricultural Machinery—(available only at certain institutes) training in the repair and maintenance of agricultural machinery.

2. Electricity Department:
a)   Electrical Installation—training in the installation of electrical equipment for industrial and architectural projects;

b)   Electro-Mechanics—training in the manufacturing of transformers, engine building and repair, general mechanical repair, as well as refrigeration work;

3. Auto Mechanics Section:
a)   Auto Mechanics— basic training in the maintenance and repair of vehicles, including scientific diagnostic methods;

b)   Auto Electrical—training that prepares trainees to find and repair defects in vehicles' electrical system;

c)   Diesel Mechanics—training in the repair and maintenance of diesel vehicles and the installation of diesel engines;

4. Electronics Section:
This section offers training in the use and repair of audio-visual equipment and industrial electronics machines. In addition to the above, two special one-year training courses are also offered at certain institutes: one in Electro-Mechanical Repair and Maintenance; and another in Architectural Maintenance.

Industrial education on the junior college level has expanded greatly since 1983. As of 1414 A.H./1994 A.D., there were 6 Intermediate Colleges of Technology in Saudi Arabia located in Riyadh, Jeddah, Dammam, Buraidah, Abha, and Al-Ahsa with a total enrollment of 6,648 students and 913 teachers. These colleges offer two-year programs, and students are required to complete a total of ninety-course hours.

The Intermediate College of Technology which opened in Riyadh in 1983 has five sections that offer specialty programs, namely:

1. Mechanical Technology section—programs on production engineering;

2. Electrical Technology section—programs in electrical installations and electrical equipment;

3. Electronic Technology section—programs in industrial electronics and automatic control;

4. Oil and Minerals Technology section—programs in industrial chemistry;

5. Auto/Engine Technology section—programs in auto mechanics and electrical systems.

Since 1989 the Junior College of Technology in Riyadh has also offered a four-year program leading to the bachelor of science degree in Technology Engineering. This degree is equivalent to those granted by other four-year colleges of engineering in Saudi Arabia.

The Colleges of Technology in Jeddah, Dammam and Buraidah each have four sections that offer programs in the following areas:

1. Mechanical Technology section—programs in production engineering, and air conditioning and refrigeration;

2. Electrical Technology section—programs in electrical installations;

3. Electronic Technology section—programs in industrial electronics;

4. Auto/Engine Technology section—programs in auto mechanics.

The two new junior colleges in Abha and Al-Ahsa offer some unique programs designed particularly to meet government sector needs for technicians, as follows:

The Junior College for Technology in Abha —

1. Electronic Technology section—offers programs in computer technology;

2. Construction Technology section—offers programs in architectural drawing;

3. Commerce and Management Technology section -offers programs in office management and computerized accounting.

The Junior College of Technology in Al-Ahsa —

1. Mechanical Technology section—offers programs in pneumatic/hydraulic control technology;

2. Electronic Technology section—offers programs in computer technology;

3. Auto/Engine Technology section—offers programs in auto control and safety;

4. Commerce and Management section—offers programs in office management and computerized accounting.

Other benefits all trainees receive are specialized books along with the earlier mentioned housing, meals, daily transportation, monthly stipend, and comprehensive medical and social services. Graduates of the technical colleges are awarded the Junior University Certificate and are given a 6.4 grade level of the civil service. Government-sponsored vocational loans are also available to graduates seeking to start their own businesses.

All Junior Colleges of Technology have the following admission requirements:

1. Trainees must be Saudi citizens. Non-Saudis may be accepted under special circumstances.

2. All trainees must have one of the following certificates:

TABLE 10-A
Total Number of Schools, Students, Teachers and Classes at the Technical Education Level, for School Years, 1404 & 1414 A.H.

LEVEL		YEAR	SCHOOLS	STUDENTS	CLASSES
HIGH	Intermediate College of Technology	1404	4	424	20
		1414	6	6648	—
SECONDARY	Secondary Industrial Institutes	1404	8	3698	175
		1414	8	8672	439
	Secondary Commercial Institutes	1404	10	6479	273
		1414	15	10335	364
	Secondary Agricultural Institutes	1404	1	145	10
		1414	3	774	37
	Secondary Technical Assistants Inst.	1404	3	398	27
		1414	5	1610	75
	TOTAL	1404	26	11144	505
		1414	37	28039	915

TABLE 10-B
Total Number of Teachers at the Technical Education level, by Saudi and/or Non-Saudi, for School Years 1404 & 1414 A.H.

LEVEL		YEAR	SAUDI	NON SAUDI	TOTAL
HIGH	Intermediate College of Technology	1404	23	53	76
		1414	464	449	913
SECONDARY	Secondary Industrial Institutes	1404	379	266	645
		1414	632	494	1126
	Secondary Commercial Institutes	1404	40	456	496
		1414	470	190	660
	Secondary Agricultural Institutes	1404	23	19	42
		1414	76	18	94
	Technical Assistants' Institutes	1404	6	81	87
		1414	100	140	240
TOTAL		1404	471	875	1346
		1414	1742	1291	3033

Sources for Tables 10-A & 10-B:
1. Ministry of Finance and National Economy, 1404 A.H.
2. General Organization for Technical Education and Vocational Training. Statistical Report for Year 1414 A.H.

    A. GOTEVT Secondary Institutes Certificate
    B. Secondary School Certificate (scientific section)
    C. Secondary School Certificate (liberal arts section)

3. The minimum requirement for trainee's grades from previous school is "Good".

4. Trainees must pass a medical exam.

5. Trainees must pass a personal interview.

6. Trainees must have received a Good Behavior Certificate from the last school they attended.

7. All trainees must enroll as full-time students.

8. No more than five years should have elapsed since receiving a secondary level certificate.

9. If three or more years have elapsed since receiving a secondary level certificate, trainees must pass a written examination supervised by a college committee.

The Higher Technical Institute in Riyadh was founded in 1982 and originally offered two and three-year training programs for instructors needed in the secondary industrial institutes and vocational training centers. Much of this education is now provided by the junior college level programs in the six colleges of technology. Currently the Higher Technical Institute offers a one-year program for College of Technology graduates which qualifies them for teaching at secondary industrial institutes, vocational centers or colleges of technology.

Between 1980-1988 there were 228 graduates from the Higher Technical Institute specializing in five fields: electrical equipment, electrical installations, auto mechanics, industrial electronics and production engineering. Trainees and graduates are granted several important benefits such as appointment of grade 6 level in the Civil Service and are paid at this level throughout their study at the Institute. Trainees who graduate as instructors are then appointed to grade 6.4 of the Civil Service and receive the corresponding pay increase. Instructors are granted an extra Higher Technical Institute monetary allowance which continues until they reach grade 7 in the Civil Service. Graduates are offered 20 percent of their salaries as a teaching allowance; this is increased to 30 percent after five years. Graduates are also granted a technical allowance for equipment and materials. In addition, instructors who graduate from the Higher Technical Institute are eligible for special training courses abroad which are paid for by the government.

Admission to the Higher Technical Institute requires that trainees possess a College of Technology Certificate and that they also pass a personal interview, admission test, and medical examination. All trainees must be Saudi citizens.

TECHNICAL COMMERCIAL EDUCATION

Commercial education programs focus on training students for a broad assortment of office, commercial and financial subjects such as accounting, bookkeeping, secretarial skills, commercial correspondence, typing, computers, and administration. The commercial institutes are located in urban areas of the Kingdom and offer three-year programs with both morning and evening classes.

In addition to the standard benefits for secondary level programs mentioned earlier, graduates of the secondary commercial institutes are appointed to grade 5 level of the Civil Service. Graduates are also eligible to continue their education at the Higher Commercial Institute or, a junior technology college, or a regular university. To be admitted to a secondary commercial institute applicants must fulfill the following requirements in addition to the standard ones. Applicants must possess an Intermediate School Certificate, pass a personal interview, and have good manual dexterity and eyesight. It is also required that students be between the ages of fifteen and eighteen to attend morning classes.

The first Higher Institute for Financial and Commercial Studies was established in Riyadh in 1975 with the second Institute opening in 1977 in Jeddah. These institutes offer morning and evening classes devoted especially to upgrading the skills and productivity of current and prospective government employees. The two-year programs qualify specialists in two general fields:

1. Business Administration and Secretarial Skills-where industrial management, social insurance, personnel affairs, purchasing, warehouse management are taught;

2. Accounting and Financial Affairs—students are taught accounting and financial principles and procedures so that they will be able to handle a variety of accounts such as banking accounts, government accounts, cost accounts and oil accounts.

In addition to the standard benefits, the graduates of the Higher Institute for Financial and Commercial Studies are eligible for government employment. The graduates also receive credit for two years of service on their work records, earn the right to promotion and have priority for continuing their education in special training courses abroad.

Admission to the higher institutes requires that applicants possess a Secondary Commercial School Certificate. A Secondary School Certificate is acceptable for enrollment in the business administration and secretarial skills section only. In addition to the appropriate certificate, applicants must fulfill the specific subject prerequisites established by GOTEVT. Applicants must also meet the standard requirements listed above and pass a personal interview.

As shown in Table 10-A, the number of secondary commercial institutes increased from 10 institutes in 1404 A.H./1984 to 15 in 1413 A.H./1993 A.D. Increases were also made in student enrollment and the number of teachers, as well as student-teacher ratio: student enrollment, from 6,479 to 8,501 and the number of teachers, from 496 to 608; and the student-teacher ratio from 13:1 to approximately 14:1, respectively.

TECHNICAL AGRICULTURAL EDUCATION

Trainees at the Agricultural Institute receive the standard benefits and, yearly, a round trip ticket to home regions. Graduates are also eligible for specialized work opportunities and job counseling and are appointed to the grade 5 level of the Civil Service.

In addition to the standard criteria, admission to the Model Agricultural Institute requires that applicants possess an Intermediate School Certificate and be at least twenty years old.

The Model Agricultural Institute in Buraidah, which opened in 1977, provides a three-year secondary level program focusing on agricultural development and farm management. Specialized courses in the following two fields are offered:

1. Agricultural Production—wherein students are educated on subject matters such as water, irrigation and drainage, land reclamation, crops, horticulture, pasturage, plant protection, plant nutrition, and bee farming;

2. Animal Production—wherein students are taught pisciculture (fish culture), milk production, poultry, meat production, animal production such as goat, camel and horse breeding, animal health, animal and poultry nutrition.

Table 10-A indicates that in 1414 A.H./1994 A.D. there was a sharp increase in student enrollment in the three secondary agricultural institutes, from 145 students in 1404 A.H./1984 A.D. to 774 students in 1414 A.H./1994 A.D.—or the equivalent of a 433% increase. There was also an increase in the number of teachers in the same eleven-year period from 42 in 1404 A.H./1984 A.D. to 94 teachers in 1414 A.H./1994 A.D.—or approximately 123% increase.

SECONDARY TECHNICAL ASSISTANTS' INSTITUTE

The Secondary Technical Assistants' Institute provide training in a variety of trades and are located in Riyadh, Abha, and Tabuk. They offer three-year programs which can be tailored to the needs of individual trainees. Graduates are awarded the Technical Supervisors Diploma.

The Secondary Technical Assistants' Institute in Riyadh offers courses in seven fields: surveying, sanitation and public health inspection, construction, water supply, architectural drawing, hydrology, and road construction. The institute in Abha offers programs in construction, architectural drawing, sanitation and public health inspection and surveying. The institute in Tabuk has the following sections: construction, surveying, and architectural drawing.

Trainees are given a monthly stipend that continues through the summer vacation during which students get practical experience working in different municipalities throughout the Kingdom. Institute graduates are appointed to grade 5 of the Civil Service.

To be admitted to a technical supervisors institute, applicants must be at least fifteen years old and pass a personal interview and an admissions test. In addition to the standard requirements, applicants must possess an Intermediate School Certificate. Citizens of any (GCC) Gulf Corporation Council member country may also be admitted. The number of Secondary Technical Assistants' Institutes, as shown in Table 10-A, remained constant at 3 over the 10-year period. However, student enrollment and the number of teachers increased from 398 students in 1404 A.H./1984 A.D. to 1,498 students in 1413 A.H./1993 A.D.—or an increase of 276%; and from 87 teachers in 1404 A.H./1984 A.D. to 222 teachers in 1413 A.H./1993 A.D.—or 155%, respectively.

VOCATIONAL AND PRE-VOCATIONAL TRAINING CENTERS

By 1413 A.H./1993 A.D. there were 325 vocational training institutes and centers offering 791 classes in morning and evening programs to students in all regions of the Kingdom (as shown in Table 11-A.) Table 11-B shows that enrollment reached 35,288 with 2,813 teachers. GOTEVT has established the following objectives for vocational training programs:

1. To qualify workers to meet industrial requirements;

2. To upgrade unskilled workers into a technically proficient work—force that relies on various trades for its livelihood;

3. To provide work opportunities for people with limited education;

4. To provide opportunities for workers to study at vocational training centers;

5. To foster moral and religious values in trainees and encourage respect for manual and vocational work;

6. To qualify the work force to meet the technical requirements of industry.

These centers' vocational orientation program combines audio-visual presentations and short, hands-on basic skills courses in order to survey different trades and help new trainees decide which ones to study. The morning and evening courses at these centers offer a variety of trades with the morning programs generally running for twelve to eighteen months and offering the following subjects: auto mechanics, refrigeration and air conditioning, general mechanics, painting and auto body repair, general electricity, radio and television repair, sheet metal, office machine repair, carpentry, plumbing, printing, welding, aluminum construction and repair, commercial and office work, diesel mechanics, etc.

Study in the pre-vocational training centers lasts for ten continuous months. The courses are meant for those who are 14-17 years old and have completed the 4th grade level of elementary school. The trades taught include machine trades, welding, carpentry, electricity, auto mechanics, typing, accounting and bookkeeping, secretarial, office work, purchasing, and store management.

Trainees receive a monthly stipend which increases after successful completion of the first half of the training program. They also receive a monetary award upon graduation, and those who achieve an excellent rating receive a bonus equivalent to an additional fifty percent of the graduation award. Graduates receive another monetary award equivalent to 150 percent of the initial graduation payment after completing six months of employment in their trade. While engaged in their studies, trainees also receive the standard benefits of free housing, food, transportation, and uniforms. The training centers provide all necessary raw materials and equipment for programs in each trade. Trainees are eligible for work opportunities in government departments; and after three years of work experience in a trade, graduates can apply for government-sponsored loans to open a private business.

Admission to the day classes at the Vocational Training Centers requires applicants to have at least a sixth-grade (elementary level) education, be in good health and without any disabilities. Applicants should also be between the ages of fifteen and forty-five and without any prior vocational courses. All applicants must be Saudi citizens.

The evening classes are generally offered over a six-month period. The trades available for study are: auto mechanics, plumbing, electrical installations, refrigeration and air conditioning, lathe operation, welding (oxygen and acetylene), carpentry and architecture, sheet metal, painting and auto body repair, and aluminum construction and repair.

Trainees receive the standard benefits listed above, and upon graduation they are given monetary awards. Admission requirements for the evening classes are the same as those for the day classes. The minimum educational requirement has been lowered, however, in terms of grade level and age.

The Instructor Training Institute offers a ten-month program to prepare Vocational Training Center graduates for further training in the United Kingdom. Only the best qualified graduates who have gained extra practical skills by working as assistant instructors are eligible for this program. The objectives of the Institute are as follows:

1. To train Saudi instructors to teach in the trade programs available in the Vocational Training Centers.

2. To upgrade the competence of instructors and technicians in various trades through in-service courses.

3. To develop and select new training curriculum materials and establish vocational training programs that strive to meet industrial requirements.

4. To conduct research and update training curricula regularly.

ON-THE-JOB TRAINING

A special department devoted to on-the-job training was established within GOTEVT in 1974 to develop programs designed to upgrade the skills of Saudi workers employed in the private sector. In conjunction with these efforts, the Council of Ministers passed a resolution in 1976 establishing training subsidies for private companies that wish to conduct training seminars for Saudi workers in order to enhance the qualifications of the work force and to help Saudi employees stay apace with the developments in modern technology.

The primary goals of the on-the-job training department are: 1) to establish local or international standards in different trades; and 2) to provide the private sector with model training programs designed to ensure and upgrade workers' skills. Various sections within the department attend to program development, research, administration, industrial guidance, and vocational testing.

TABLE 11-A
Total Number of Schools, Students, and Classes at the Vocational Education level, for School Years 1404 & 1413 A.H.

LEVEL		YEAR	SCHOOLS	STUDENTS	CLASSES
VOCATIONAL EDUCATION	Vocational Training Center (VTC)	1404	57	7126	141
		1413	54	9512	332
	On-The-Job Training Program (OJT)	1404	3	159	—
		1413	3	466	—
	Health Institutes	1404	11	1732	100
		1413	42	5110	261
	Sewing Centers	1404	15	1284	101
		1413	25	1726	140
	Postal and Telecommunications Institutes	1404	9	1693	109
		1413	10	937	53
	Veterinary and Animal Husbandry Institutes	1404	1	25	3
		1413	1	93	5
	Other Training	1404	58	9453	227
		1413	41	386	—
	Training in the Private Sector	1404	44	5469	188
		1413	149	17508	—
TOTAL		1404	198	26941	869
		1413	325	35288	791

Sources:
1. Ministry of Finance and National Economy, 1404 A.H.
2. Ministry of Education and General Presidency of Girls' Education Statistical Charts for School Year 1413 A.H.

TABLE 11-B
Total Number of Teachers at the Vocational Education level, by Saudi and/or Non-Saudi, for School Years 1404 & 1413 A.H.

LEVEL		YEAR	SAUDI	NON SAUDI	TOTAL
VOCATIONAL EDUCATION	Vocational Trainig Center (VTC	1404	792	524	1316
		1413	872	546	1418
	On-The-Job Training Program (OJT)	1404	18	—	18
		1413	73	23	96
	Health Institutes	1404	61	210	271
		1413	271	464	735
	Sewing Centers	1404	110	85	195
		1413	162	106	268
	Postal and Telecommunications Institutes	1404	91	242	333
		1413	137	125	262
	Veterinary and Animal Husbandry Institutes	1404	3	8	11
		1413	9	2	11
	Other Training	1404	705	528	1233
		1413	23	—	23
	Training in the Private Sector	1404	9	25	34
		1413	—	—	—
	TOTAL	1404	1789	1622	3411
		1413	1547	1266	2813

Sources:
1. Ministry of Finance and National Economy, 1404 A.H.
2. Ministry of Education and General Presidency of Girls' Education Statistical Charts for School Year 1413 A.H.

The objectives of the on-the-job training programs are as follows:

1. To train Saudi staff members to obtain on-the-job training skills so they can develop relevant programs and curricula.

2. To train Saudi supervisors to administer these programs and to oversee the training staff.

3. To continue the support and expansion of services and financial incentives for private sector companies that offer on-the-job training programs to their employees.

4. To develop a system of technical and vocational testing and certification in order to set a standard of performance for skilled and semi-skilled workers in different trades.

5. To train government technicians.

6. To work cooperatively with GOTE √T training and educational departments and the private sector to develop the skills of the national work force.

All on-the-job training programs and their participants are registered with the department. Staff members advise the companies about the programs that they have and what is best suited to their needs. Program participants must be Saudi citizens; preference is given to those who can read and write and who are under forty-five years of age. Financial subsidies are available for training programs given at company locations in the Kingdom and abroad. Program trainees are paid salaries or stipends while studying and also receive allowances for books, medical expenses, and other program-related costs. On-the-job training programs have been integrated into fields such as industrial relations, gas and electric utilities, fisheries, cable manufacturing, pneumatics, and steel manufacturing.

Although the number of on-the-job training centers remained constant at three in the eleven-year period, 1404 A.H./1984 A.D. to 1414 A.H./1994 A.D., the number of students in this program increased by 193%, from 159 students in 1404 A.H./1984 A.D. to 466 students in 1414 A.H./1994 A.D. The number of teachers also registered an increase of about 433%, from 18 in 1404 A.H./1984 A.D. to 96 in 1414 A.H./1994 A.D.

COOPERATIVE EDUCATION

In addition to on-the-job training programs, GOTEVT has developed close cooperative education programs with many industries that allow employees to further their skills by studying at government institutes. Over the last decade, about 35 percent of GOTEVT students have benefited from such cooperative arrangements.

There are two types of training programs in the field of technical education: a short one-year course that offers basic training in mechanics and electricity, and a three-year general course that offers the full curricula of technical education. Students working in several industrial sectors have taken advantage of cooperative education opportunities in a variety of fields such as manufacturing, oil, electric power, and aviation.

Cooperative education in vocational fields is also served by some private institutes that are licensed by the government. The programs offered at these institutes are evaluated by GOTEVT and include training in the following areas:

1. Administration and commercial education - typing, secretarial skills, accounting, administration and supervision, marketing, shorthand, telex, and computers;

2. Other technical and vocational fields - industrial safety and security, electronics, machine operation and maintenance, interior decoration, radio and television repair, surveying and architectural drawing, aviation services and tourism, printing, air conditioning repair, production engineering and mechanics.

Cooperative agreements have also been forged with foreign governments and international organizations that provide opportunities to study certain fields abroad. These agreements include programs for trainees to study 1) industrial education in France; 2) engineering, instructor training, and industrial and agricultural equipment in Germany; 3) vocational training in the United States; and 4) industrial electronics, telecommunications, audio-visual electronics, and computer technology in Japan.

The integrated system of technical education and vocational training in Saudi Arabia provides extensive opportunities for workers to learn new skills and enter a new, technologically sophisticated work-force. These programs enable Saudi workers to help shape their nation's future development in business, industry, and agriculture.

5. FOURTH LEVEL—HIGHER EDUCATION

Higher education in Saudi Arabia is a function of the central government. It is planned, funded, and administered by the central government's Ministry of Higher Education established in 1975. It is the responsibility of the Ministry to make higher education accessible to every Saudi citizen who desires it and is able to fulfill the basic admission requirements.

The Ministry proposes educational institutions and authorizes them to offer specified programs of instruction in accordance with standards established by the government. This system provides a means for the establishment of standards and national uniformity. In addition to the creation and administration of colleges and universities in the Kingdom, the Ministry also maintains the educational missions in 32 countries. These missions are responsible for the education of Saudi students in the respective countries.

The postsecondary system of education in Saudi Arabia is, to a significant extent, based upon the educational system in the United States, with many modifications taken from the British, French, German, Italian, and Egyptian systems. The patterns and procedures from these educational systems have been combined with the age-old Islamic systems, its traditions and customs.

The colleges and universities were established in accordance with the needs of the country. The academic programs at any of the seven universities are first initiated at the departmental, college, and university levels. The recommended programs are then forwarded to the Supreme Council of the United Saudi Universities of the Ministry of Higher Education. Although the Ministry of Higher Education has the final approval of academic programs, the approval of the Council of Ministers is essential for the development of new institutions.

Prior to the establishment of the Ministry of Higher Education in 1975, higher education in the Kingdom was largely the responsibility of the Ministry of Education. By 1975, the Ministry of Education had seven institutions under its supervision with the first institution of higher learning, King Saud University, being established in 1957. The overwhelming responsibility of one ministry was compounded by the lack of coordination among the various institutions. A report made in 1975 by a team of education experts from the United States noted the absence of coordination and communication among these independent universities. It was then recommended that better coordination be established by increasing the level of communication among the universities. The team also recommended that special care be given to higher education as it provides one of the main sources for highly skilled manpower and leads in developing the human resources of the Kingdom.

The increased responsibilities of higher education became unmanageable for the Ministry of Education. Thus, in 1975, a segment of the Ministry of Education became a separate Ministry of Higher Education with the purpose of dealing exclusively with the area of higher education. Among its responsibilities were: raising the level of communication and coordination between institutions of higher learning, coordinating with other governmental ministries and agencies in terms of their interests and needs in higher education, and acted as change agents that could help guide the country's continuing development.

A Supreme Council for Universities was formed as part of the Ministry of Higher Education to serve as the legislative coordinating body for all universities. However, to enhance the fast development of higher education over the years, a Royal Decree was issued in 1413 A.H./1993 A.D. approving the Higher Education Council and Universities system.

The Higher Education Council is the supreme authority for post-secondary education affairs with the specific task of supervising and coordinating its institutions with the sole exception of military education. The Council's responsibilities include: directing university education in accordance with the drawn policy, supervising the development of university education in all sectors, coordinating among universities especially in the field of scientific departments and degrees, encouraging research, formulating rules and regulations for compliance by all institutions of higher learning, among others.

The Prime Minister who is also the chairman of the High Committee on Education Policies is the chairman of the Higher Education Council with the Minister of Higher Education as deputy chairman. Other members of the Council include the Ministers of Education, Finance & National Economy, Labor & Social Affairs, and Planning, the Chairman of the General Civil Service Board, the General President of Girls' Education and the university rectors. A secretary general for the Council for Higher Education is appointed by the chairman of the Council to assume the duties of the Council secretariat and preparing its tasks.

Each university is run by its University Council, university rector and deputy rectors. Each of these councils is composed of the following: the Minister of Higher Education as chairman and the university rector as deputy chairman, deputy rectors, the secretary general of the Higher Education Council, the deans of all colleges within the university and three experienced persons appointed by the Minister of Higher Education for a period of three (3) years.

The University Council handles educational administrative and financial affairs and implement the general policy of the university such as establishing criteria, procedures and means of carrying out the policies on higher education within the institutional boundaries and preparing future study plans and budget proposals.

A Scientific Council is set up in each university to encourage and supervise scientific and research studies and publications. The Scientific Council consists of the following: Deputy Rector for Post-Graduate Studies and Scientific Research as chairman, and a staff member from each faculty or institute with the degree of professor who are appointed by the university council on the basis of recommendations by the faculty or institute council and with the approval of the university rector.

Within the university, each college has its own council. The college council consists of the dean, the department chairmen, and selected faculty members with the following responsibilities: to implement and carry the university's objectives within the college, to operate under the university's policies and regulations and to prepare proposals for future plans and to prepare the budget requests which must be presented to the university board for review and approval.

Within the departmental level, another council exists and is headed by the chairperson and includes all faculty as its members. This council is charged with the responsibility of reviewing and updating the curricula, preparing proposals for innovations and expansion as well as future projects that the department needs.

Higher education in Saudi Arabia has undergone tremendous growth over the last three decades. The higher education system, which is based on diversification, has expanded to include seven major universities, eleven girls' colleges, and an Armed Forces Command and Staff College that offer a comprehensive variety of academic specialties. There are junior colleges that prepares teachers for the labour market. The universities and colleges offer graduate studies programs such as the Master's and Doctorate degrees in certain fields. Tables 12-A, 12-B and 12-C below show the development of higher education over a nine-year period, from 1402 A.H./1982 A.D. to 1411 A.H./1991 A.D. Specifically, while Table 12-A provides a rundown of the number of colleges, students and teachers in the seven universities and girls' colleges, Tables 12-B & 12-C show a breakdown of the colleges, student enrollment and teacher population into male and female categories. Following are the profiles of the seven universities:

1. *King Saud University* — Formerly known as the Riyadh University, and returned to its original name of King Saud University (KSU), it is the oldest university in the Kingdom and was founded in 1957. It represents Saudi Arabia's first commitment to the development of higher education. Considered the largest university in the Kingdom, KSU registered a 46% increase in student enrollment over a ten-year period, from 20,883 students in 1404 A.H./1984 A.D. to 30,559 students in 1413 A.H./1993 A.D. Its faculty increased in the same period, from 2,346 in 1404 A.H./ 1984 A.D. to 2,696 in 1413 A.H./1993 A.D., or by 15%, as shown in Table 12-A. School year 1989-90 saw the graduation of 3,952 students of which 3,127 were Saudis—2,451 male Saudis and 676 female Saudis. KSU had an annual budget of SR 5.4 million or US$1.48 million in 1960 which has increased immensely since then to SR1,505,000,000 or US $400 million in 1990-91. (Ministry of Higher Education, 1990/91, p.4)

King Saud University colleges, with branches in Abha and Al-Qaseem, offers 123 undergraduate majors and graduate degrees in 21 academic majors. The graduate program started with two students in 1977-78 which increased to 10 students in the doctorate level, and 298 master's level in 1990/1991. Within the King Saud University are the following colleges and institutes: Arabic Language Institute, Institute of Languages & Translations, College of Administrative Sciences, College of Allied Medical Sciences, College of Agriculture, College of Agriculture and Veterinary Medicine (in Qaseem), College of Arts, College of Business and Economics (in Qaseem), College of Computer and Information Sciences, College of Dentistry, College of Education, College of Education (in Abha), College of Engineering, College of Medicine, College of Medicine (in Abha), College of Pharmacy, College of Planning and Architectural Design, College of Sciences, The Graduate School. These are all for male students.

Also included within the KSU are the colleges for women, namely: The Center for University Studies for Women — College of Administrative Sciences, College of Agriculture, College of Allied Medical Sciences, College of Arts, College of Dentistry, College of Education, College of Medicine, College of Pharmacy, College of Science.

2. *KING ABDULAZIZ UNIVERSITY* — King Abdulaziz University (KAU) which is the second largest university in the Kingdom, located in Jeddah, was founded by local businessmen in 1387/1388 A.H. (1967/1968 A.D.). In 1391/1392 A.H. (1971/1972), KAU became a state-run institution.

The academic programs at KAU are similar to those at King Saud University. KAU focuses on the sciences, medicine, economics and humanities. In addition, it has a faculty for navigational sciences reflecting Jeddah's geographic location on the Red Sea.

Table 12-A shows that 33,037 students attended the King Abdulaziz University in 1413 A.H./1993 A.D. which had a faculty of about 1,987. Two thousand four hundred fourteen (2,414) students graduated from the KAU in the school year 1989-1990. In 1990-1991, KAU had 10 students at the doctorate level, 664 students in the master's level and 150 in the H. Diploma level. KAU also has a branch in the holy city of Madinah which specializes in teacher training. The university's initial budget of SR 6 Million (US$1.64 million) in 1970-71 has increased to its budget of SR 1,205 million or about US$321 million in 1990-91. (Ministry of Higher Education, 1990/91, p.4)

The colleges in King Abdulaziz University are the following: College of Arts and Humanities, College of Earth Sciences, College of Economics and Administration, College of Education (in Madinah), College of Engineering, College of Marine Science, College of Medicine and Medical Sciences, College of Meteorology, and College of Science.

3. *KING FAHD UNIVERSITY OF PETROLEUM AND MINERALS* — The King Fahd University of Petroleum and Minerals (KFUPM) was founded by the late King Faisal Bin Abdul Aziz in 1963. Located in the eastern city of Dhahran, it is widely acknowledged to be the leading institution for the study of energy sciences in the Middle East. The popularity of KFUPM is reflected in its steady enrollment. As shown in Table 12-A, KFUPM is one of the smallest universities in the Kingdom with a student enrollment of 4,935 in 1413 A.H./1993 A.D. from its initial enrollment of 63 students in 1963. The number of faculty in the same year registered at 695 . There were 485 graduates in 1989-1990. The number of students at the post-graduate level were as follows: doctorate—8; and master's—292. The 1990-1991 budget for King Fahd University was SR 350,950,000 or about US$ 93.6 million. (Ministry of Higher Education, 1990/91, p.4)

TABLE 12-A
Total Number of Colleges, Students, and Teachers at the Higher Education level, for School Years 1404 & 1413 A.H.

UNIVERSITIES	COLLEGES		STUDENTS		TEACHERS	
	1404	1413	1404	1413	1404	1413
Imam Moh.Ibn Saud Islamic University	13	13	10860	20734	987	1263
Islamic University	6	5	3334	3058	378	378
King Abdulaziz University	9	9	18698	33037	1413	1987
King Faisal University	6	6	2631	5240	601	727
King Fahd Univ. of Petro.& Minerals	5	8	3814	4935	679	695
King Saud University	15	17	20883	30559	2346	2696
Umm Al Qura University	6	9	8271	18635	998	1184
Girls' Colleges	11	14	11730	19582	980	1186
T O T A L	71	81	80221	135780	8382	10116

Sources: Ministry of Finance and National Economy, 1404 and 1413 A.H.

TABLE 12-B

Total Number of Colleges and Students at the Higher Education level, by Boys & Girls, for School Years 1404 & 1413 A.H.

UNIVERSITIES	COLLEGES						STUDENTS				
	1404			1413			1404		1413		
	BOYS	GIRLS	UNSPEC	BOYS	GIRLS	UNSPEC	BOYS	GIRLS	BOYS	GIRLS	
Imam Moh.Ibn Saud Islamic Univ.	4	9	0	7	6	0	9303	1557	17568	3166	
Islamic University	6	0	0	5	—	0	3334	—	3058	0	
King Abdulaziz University	4	5	0	4	5	0	13041	5657	20403	12634	
King Fah d Univ.Petro.& Min.	6	0	0	8	—	0	3814	—	4935	0	
King Faisal University	1	4	0	2	4	0	1607	1024	2553	2687	
King Saud University	5	10	0	6	11	—	16366	4517	19808	10751	
Umm Al Qura University	0	6	0	1	8	0	4158	4113	10327	8308	
Girls' Colleges	0	0	11	0	—	14	—	11730	0	19582	
T O T A L	26	34	11	33	34	14	51623	28598	78652	57128	
GRAND TOTAL	71			81			80,221		135,780		

Source: Ministry of Finance and National Economy, 1404 and 1413 A.H.

TABLE 12-C
Total Number of Faculty at the Higher Education level, by Saudi or Non-Saudi, for School Years 1404 & 1413 A.H.

UNIVERSITIES		1404				1413			
		MALE	FEMALE	TOTAL	G.TOTAL	MALE	FEMALE	TOTAL	G.TOTAL
Imam Moh.Ibn Saud Islamic Univ.	S	562	—	562	987	792	5	797	1,263
	NS	425	—	425		465	1	466	
Islamic University	S	165	—	165	378	337	0	337	378
	NS	213	—	213		41	0	41	
King Abdulaziz University	S	429	176	605	1413	926	385	1311	1,987
	NS	643	165	808		494	182	676	
King Fahd Univ.Petro.& Min.	S	202	—	202	601	228	0	228	695
	NS	399	—	399		466	1	467	
King Faisal University	S	294	—	294	679	322	84	406	727
	NS	385	—	385		264	57	321	
King Saud University	S	685	120	805	2346	955	241	1196	2,696
	NS	1265	276	1541		1178	322	1500	
Umm Al Qura University	S	426	119	545	998	555	149	704	1,184
	NS	376	77	453		401	79	480	
Girls' Colleges	S	1	339	340	980	1	600	601	1,186
	NS	49	591	640		169	416	585	
T O T A L		6519	1863	8382		7594	2522	10,116	

Sources: Ministry of Finance and National Economy, 1404 & 1413 A.H.

As the leading center for scientific research and innovation, KFUPM plays a major and pioneering role in the Kingdom's development efforts. In 1985, KFUPM's Research Institute undertook 74 projects for government and scientific agencies. The technological sophistication of KFUPM was demonstrated by the participation of KFUPM Research Institute scientists in preparation for Prince Sultan Bin Salman's June 1985 journey aboard the space shuttle Discovery.

The university has the following colleges: College of Applied Engineering, College of Engineering Science, College of Environmental Design, College of Graduate Studies, College of Industrial Management, College of Sciences.

4. *ISLAMIC UNIVERSITY* — Founded in 1961 as a traditional Islamic institution, the Islamic University in Madinah has a diverse student and teaching body coming from Islamic and other countries worldwide. Reorganized in 1975 to respond to the developmental needs of Saudi Arabia and other Muslim countries, it is presently under the direct supervision of the Council of Ministers. Students at the university study for degrees in the fields of linguistics and Islamic Literature in the College of Arabic Language, College of Dawa and Usul-Ad-Din, and in the fields of Islamic Law and Quranic Studies in the College of Hadith & Islamic Studies, College of Holy Qur'an & Islamic Studies, College of Sharia and Section of Higher Studies. Table 12-A shows an 8% decrease in student enrollment, or from 3,334 in 1404 A.H./1984 A.D. to 3,058 students in 1413 A.H./1993 A.D. with the number of faculty remaining unchanged at 378. Four hundred seventy-three students graduated in 1989-1990 of which 147 were male Saudis. Total number of students at the post-graduate level were as follows—doctorate: 131; and master's: 149. The 1990-1991 budget for the Islamic University was SR 197,585,000 or US$ 52.6 million. (Ministry of Higher Education, 1990/91, p. 4)

5. *IMAM MUHAMMAD BIN SAUD ISLAMIC UNIVERSITY* — The Imam Muhammad Bin Saud Islamic University, founded in 1974, is a consolidation of a number of scientific and Islamic institutes located in Riyadh and other cities in Saudi Arabia. The Scientific Institute of Riyadh, established by the late King Abdul Aziz in 1950, forms the core of what is now known as Imam Muhammad Bin Saud University.

The university's local branches in Madinah, Abha, and Al-Hasa which specializes in Islamic studies, such as Sharia (Islamic Law), Usul Din (Islamic Theology) and Dawa (Islamic mission); teacher education; and Arabic language and literature accept foreign students from 106 Arab, African, Asian and European countries. Overseas, it has affiliations with the Islamic and Arabic institutes located in Mauritania, Djibouti and Ras

Al-Khaima in the United Arab Emirates. In addition to these, it operates three Arabic language institutes in Japan, Indonesia and the U.S.A. Following are the colleges within the university: Higher Institute of Qadha'* in Riyadh, Higher Institute of Islamic Dawa in Madinah, College of Sharia in Riyadh, Arabic Language College in Riyadh, Usul Ad Din College in Riyadh, Ad Dawa Wa Al E'Elam** College in Riyadh, Social Science College in Riyadh, A Sharia Wa Usul Ad Din College in Qaseem and the Southern province, Arabic and Social Science College in Qaseem and the Southern Province, A Sharia and Islamic Studies College in Al Hasa, Institute of Learning Arabic Language in Riyadh, Girls' Study Center in Riyadh.

The growth of the university reflects the development of higher education in Saudi Arabia. As shown in Tables 12-A and 12-B, student enrollment increased by 91%, from 10,860 in 1404 A.H./1984 A.D. to 20,734 in 1413 A.H./1993 A.D. And of the 20,734 students, 17,568 were males and 3,166 were females. The number of faculty also increased, by 28% or 1,263, over the same period. In 1990-1991, there were 264 students at the doctorate level, 487 at the master's level and 61 at the H. Diploma level. School year 1989-1990 witnessed the graduation of 2,049 students from the Imam Mohammed Bin Saud Islamic University. Budget for the school year 1990-1991 was SR 1,048,707,453 or US$280 million.(Ministry of Higher Education, 1990/91, p.4)

6. *KING FAISAL UNIVERSITY* — King Faisal University (KFU) was established in 1975 in Al-Hasa in the Eastern Province. It offers degrees relating to agriculture, education, veterinary sciences, and medicine in its colleges, namely: College of Administrative Science and Planning, College of Agriculture and Food Science, College of Architecture and Planning (in Dammam), College of Education, College of Medicine and Medical Sciences, and College of Veterinary Medicine. Student enrollment, which totalled 2,631 in 1404 A.H./1984 A.D. increased by 99%, or 5,240, in 1413 A. H./1993 A.D. And the number of faculty increased by 21% over the same period, as shown in Table 12-A. Table 12-B indicates that there were 134 more female than male students: 2,553 male students and 2,687 female students. There were 748 students who graduated in 1989-1990 from King Faisal University. The total number of students in the post-graduate level in 1990-91 were as follows: doctorate level—149; and master's level—112. The annual budget for 1990-91 was SR 350,000,000 or US$93.3 million. (Ministry of Higher Education, 1990/91, p.4)

In addition to the above mentioned academic areas KFU also offers

---

*Qadha, also pronounced as Qadaa' means judiciary.
**Al Dawa Wa Al E'Elam means Information and Communication or Mass Communications.

degrees in foreign languages, chemistry, mathematics, social sciences and education. Also, KFU's 380-bed teaching hospital maintains an active exchange program with hospitals and medical schools overseas.

7. *UMM AL-QURA UNIVERSITY* — The most recent addition to the universities in the Kingdom is the Umm Al-Qura University which is located in the holy city of Makkah and is composed of some of the Kingdom's oldest institutions of higher education. The roots of Umm Al-Qura University date back to the Sharia College, founded in 1949 and the Teachers' College established in 1952. These two colleges were combined in 1960-61 to become the College of Sharia and Education. In 1971, the college became affiliated with the King Abdulaziz University in Jeddah. In 1980, a Royal decree established the college as an independent university, renaming it Umm Al-Qura University. In 1404 A.H./1984 A.D. student enrollment totalled 8,271. Table 12-A shows that this number increased by 125%, or 18,635, in 1413 A.H./1993 A.D.in its nine academic colleges and Arabic language institute as well as its branch in Taif. Although the focus of the university is on religion, teacher education and the sciences have become popular with students. The number of faculty in this university totalled 1,184 in 1413 A.H./1993 A.D. In 1989-1990, 2,165 students graduated from this university. Its graduate program has a sizeable student population, as follows: doctorate level—304; master's level—1,111 and H. Diploma level—267. Total annual budget for this university in 1990-91 was SR 546,373,000 or US$ 145.7 million. (Ministry of Higher Education, 1990/91, p.4)

8. *GIRLS' COLLEGES*
   The eleven Girls' Colleges are the following:
   College of Arts (Riyadh), founded in 1979;
   College of Arts (Dammam), founded in 1979;
   College of Education (Riyadh), founded in 1970
   College of Education (Jeddah), founded in 1974;
   College of Education (Makkah), founded in 1975;
   College of Education (Abha), founded in 1981;
   College of Education (Buraidah), founded in 1981;
   College of Education (Madinah), founded in 1981;
   College of Education (Tabuk), founded in 1982;
   College of Science (Dammam), founded in 1979; and
   College of Social Work (Riyadh) founded in 1975.

Table 12-A shows increases made in number of colleges, student enrollment and faculty in the Girls' Colleges. Student enrollment increased to 19,582 in 1413 A.H./1993 A.D. compared to its 1404 A.H./1984 A.D. figure of 11,730. While the number of colleges increased, from 11 to 14, the number of faculty also increased from 980 faculty in 1404 A.H./1984 A.D.to 1,186 faculty in 1413 A.D./1993 A.H.

Five of the above seven Saudi universities — King Saud, King Abdulaziz, King Faisal, Imam Mohammed Bin Saud Islamic and Umm Al-Qura — are co-educational while King Fahd University of Petroleum and Minerals and Islamic University are exclusively for male students only. While the Islamic University is under the direct supervision of the Council of Ministers, the other six universities fall under the auspices of the Ministry of Higher Education with the Girls' Colleges supervised by the General Presidency of Girls' Education.

Each of the institutions of higher learning is separately chartered and functions semi-autonomously, though they all share common goals of instruction, research and service. All the universities are governed by the policy developed by the Supreme Council on Universities. The Minister of Higher Education serves as the Deputy President of this Supreme Council and as the Supreme President of the seven universities. The girls' colleges are governed by policy developed by the Colleges Supreme Council, an independent body whose members, like those of the Supreme Council on Universities, include the heads of government agencies and distinguished educators.

Total enrollment in institutions of higher learning has increased dramatically. In 1969-70, male university level students totaled 6,942 which increased, approximately ten-fold, to 78,652 in 1413 A.H./1993 A.D, as shown in Table 12-B. Combining this with the enrollment of 67,128 female students, total enrollment in higher education in 1413 A.H./1993 A.D. reached 145,780. Funding allocation for higher education in 1990/91 totaled SR 6,097 million or US$1,626 million. (Ministry of Higher Education, 1990-91, p.4)

DEGREE PROGRAMS IN THE UNIVERSITIES

Two of the universities offer programs that are below the bachelor's level. These programs, like others in technical education institutes, train specialized technicians in different fields and grant terminal degrees. Applicants must possess a Secondary School Certificate for admission to these programs.

King Abdulaziz University College of Earth Science's two- year program grants diplomas in Earth Science and Geology Laboratory Assitants, while its College of Meteorology and Environmental Studies grants diplomas in Meteorology and Meteorologist Assistants.

King Saud University College of Computer and Information Sciences' two-and-a-half-year program trains students to become computer operators and awards the Diploma in Computer Technology.

Bachelor of Arts and Bachelor of Science degrees are granted at all

Saudi universities and girls' colleges and generally require four years of study. Certain subjects, such as engineering, veterinary medicine and pharmacy require longer programs:

King Fahd University of Petroleum and Minerals has a one-year preparatory program emphasizing English and four-year program for engineering;

Umm Al-Qura University has a four-year engineering program plus a two-year program of practical applications;

King Abdulaziz University has a five-year engineering program including one semester of intensive English;

King Saud University at Qaseem's Veterinary Medicine has a five-year program which awards a degree of Bachelor of Veterinary Medicine;

King Faisal University at Al-Hasa has a five-year program which grants a Bachelor's Degree in Veterinary Medicine and Animal Surgery;

King Saud University has a five-year Pharmacy program in which one year is devoted to preparatory intensive English.

Degrees in medicine and dental science require longer programs and internships and they start immediately after completion of secondary school. The Doctor of Medicine is a six-year program, including three years of clinical work and one year compulsory internship. The Doctor of Dental Science degree consists of three semesters of intensive English and general science, and a five-year program, with one-year compulsory internship.

Graduate studies beyond the bachelor's degree are offered in Education and Education Administration such as: a one-year program in education emphasizing educational methods and practical experience which trains students to become intermediate and secondary school teachers (This program accepts students who have received a bachelor's degree from colleges other than Education.); and a one-year program in educational administration which trains students to become administrators of intermediate and secondary schools. (This program accepts students who are teachers with bachelor's degrees.)

Every Saudi university and girls' college offers post-graduate programs leading to a Master's or Ph.D. degree. The graduate programs available at Saudi institutions of higher learning include Islamic studies, humanities, Arabic language, social sciences, education, engineering, earth science, industrial management and social services.

HIGHER EDUCATION FACULTY

The structure and rank of the teaching staff in Saudi universities and colleges is similar to that found in American higher education. Assistant Professors in most fields are expected to have a doctoral degree (Ph.D.) from an accredited institution. They generally have four years to submit research that will be evaluated in order to receive promotion to a rank of Associate

Professor. Associate Professors then have four years to submit further research for consideration for promotion to Full Professor.

The Saudi higher education system permits those who hold master's degrees (M.A.) to teach but it also encourages them to obtain doctoral (Ph.D.) degrees. Those who do not earn their doctoral degrees within five years are expected to leave teaching and enter administration. Professors at all levels are encouraged to be active in research, conferences, seminars, academic committees, designing curricula, and writing books. Faculty members are also urged to take their sabbaticals outside the country so that they may bring back a fresh infusion of knowledge and expertise that reflects the latest international developments in their fields.

This brief discussion of higher education in Saudi Arabia offers a glimpse of a system of universities and colleges that has seen tremendous growth in a very short period of time. Like other elements of the educational system in the Kingdom, higher education is designed and evaluated in relation to the overall national development plan and is considered essential for fulfilling the potential of the Kingdom's greatest resource — its people.

Specialized programs provide Saudi students with training in a broad array of vocations including teaching, public administration, health care and the military. The institutes and programs devoted to these fields form an important segment of the educational system, one that seeks to fulfill the need for citizens with training in specific occupations.

VI. TEACHER TRAINING

Teacher training programs have developed as an integral part of the educational system in Saudi Arabia. Over the last five decades the standards for teacher training have been rising steadily, paralleling the general development of the educational system in the Kingdom. For example, in the 1940s elementary school teachers' qualifications were limited to an Elementary Level Certificate. This requirement was upgraded to an Intermediate Level Certificate by 1953, then to a Secondary Level Certificate in 1965 and recently to a Junior College Diploma. However, with the eventual phasing out of the secondary and junior college level programs for elementary school teachers, the new minimum requirement for teaching in all education levels is a 4-year bachelor's degree.

Under the new system established to accommodate the updated requirements, secondary school graduates who earn two-year junior college degrees are qualified to become teachers' assistants. Teachers with the older, lower level training certificates can update their knowledge and qualifications in special programs offered at two teacher training centers.

The Schools of Education at Saudi universities and girls' colleges provide a broad curriculum in education theory and methods, and also have separate departments for mathematics, physics, biology, Arabic language and Islamic studies. Every student is required to have a subject specialty within one of these departments and therefore should combine courses in education with in-depth knowledge of a particular subject. Many prospective Islamic studies teachers choose to study at the schools of education located at one of the three universities that specialize in religious subjects: Imam Mohammed bin Saud Islamic University, Islamic University in Madinah, or Umm Al-Qura University. Schools of Education also offer short training programs for students who want to become teachers but who graduate with subject majors outside the education schools.

Saudi teachers are paid one third more than other professionals with comparable qualifications and have almost three months vacation during the summer. Non-Saudi teachers receive slightly lower salaries but increased benefits that include free housing, yearly round-trip transportation to and from their home countries for their entire families during summer vacation, and the same comprehensive medical care available to Saudi citizens. The children of non-Saudi teachers also receive free schooling.

JUNIOR COLLEGE TEACHER TRAINING — The new minimum requirement for teachers to have a bachelor's degree has made many of the lower level training programs obsolete. They are described here, however, because they are still in operation while being phased out gradually. These programs will not accept new students but will allow students already enrolled to complete their studies. These teacher training centers have functioned as separate institutions. Regular community-based junior colleges continue to offer a major in education, but this major does not lead to teaching certification. Upon graduating with such a major, students who want to teach must continue their schooling at a four-year college or a university.

The existing junior college level programs include one to retrain elementary school teachers who have already taught for at least three years. Applicants must pass a competitive admissions examination and possess a certificate from secondary school, a secondary teacher training institute or the equivalent. Upon graduation students receive the Diploma for Junior College Training for Teachers. Upon receipt of this diploma, women are eligible to teach in intermediate schools; men remain teachers at the elementary level.

Applicants who have certificates from secondary level divisions, physical education, art education institutes, and teacher training institutes must complete a non-credit, preparatory semester in addition to the four semesters that are required for secondary science division graduates. There are two semesters per academic year, each seventeen weeks long.

The preparatory semester consists of a total of twenty-five hours per week of coursework divided among the following areas: algebra, analytical geometry, arithmetic and geometry, biology, chemistry, physics, English, and Qur'anic studies. The main program is comprised of seventy-five semester hours of credit, thirty-eight of which are for the required courses listed below. Coursework for a major and minor is also required and students can choose from the following fields: Arabic, art education, Islamic studies, Qur'anic studies, mathematics, physical education, science, and social studies.

An "intensive program" which qualifies teachers for intermediate schools is available to junior college graduates after they teach an additional two years in elementary school. This program is offered at selected junior colleges and is two semesters long. Graduates are awarded the Certificate of Completing the Intensive Program in the field of their choice.

Junior college graduates with a minimum of a B grade average are eligible for admission to Saudi universities and receive transfer credit for all their courses.

SCIENCE AND MATHEMATICS — Originally there were four centers—one each in Riyadh, Makkah, Taif and Dammam—that trained male students to teach science and mathematics in intermediate schools for boys. These centers were reduced to two recently and are also in the process of being phased out in light of the new bachelor's degree requirement for teachers. This new higher level training will have special benefits in mathematics and science education since college and university programs can stay apace with new developments more effectively.

Applicants to the junior college level Science and Mathematics Centers must possess a Science Division Secondary School Certificate for admission. Students with certificates from a Secondary Teacher Training Institute or Secondary School Humanities Division must pass a one-semester, non-credit remedial program consisting of twenty-two course hours before they are permitted to begin the regular three-year program. Graduates of the Art or Physical Education institutes are not eligible for admission to the centers.

The first two years of the program are spent at the center studying the required subjects shown above. The third year includes internship and further study of selected subjects. Students must maintain a minimum grade point average of 2.5 in order to graduate.

Students are awarded the Diploma for Science and Mathematics after they complete the first two years and receive the Qualification for Teaching in Intermediate Schools after the third year of the program. In 1989 there were 943 students divided among the 38 classes in the Science and Mathematics Centers. In 1990-1991, the two centers had a combined enrollment of 107 students.

ART EDUCATION— The Art Education Institute, founded in Riyadh in 1965, prepares male students to teach art at the elementary and intermediate levels. The program is at the secondary level and applicants must possess an Intermediate School Certificate for admission. Institute graduates receive a Secondary Certificate of Art Education.

The program requires three years of study and includes the subjects listed above. Institute graduates who receive a score of "Very Good" on their certificate examination and complete two years of teaching are eligible for admission to the King Saud University College of Education as Art Education majors.

TABLE 13-A
Total Number of Schools, Students, Teachers and Classes for Teachers' Institute, by Supervising Agency, for School Years 1404 & 1414 A.H.

SUPERVISING AGENCY	SCHOOLS		STUDENTS		TEACHERS		CLASSES	
	1404	1414	1404	1414	1404	1414	1404	1414
Ministry of Education	102	18	11102	17493	1505	1319	577	577
Pres. of Girls' Educ.	99	178	6289	45874	792	2566	310	581
TOTAL	201	196	17391	63367	2297	3885	887	1158

Source:
Ministry of Finance and National Economy, 1404 & 1414 A.H.

TABLE 13-B
Total Number of Teachers at the Teacher's Institute, by Saudi and/or Non-Saudi, for School Years 1404 & 1414 A.H.

NATIONALITY	1404	1413
Saudi	544	775
Non-Saudi	1753	3110
TOTAL	2297	3885

Sources:
Ministry of Finance and National Economy, 1404 & 1414 A.H.

PHYSICAL EDUCATION—The Institute of Physical Education for Men, established in Riyadh in 1964, trains male students to teach Physical Education at elementary schools for boys. It offers a three-year secondary level program that includes the subjects listed below. An Intermediate School Certificate is required for admission. The Institute is quite selective and, in the last few years, accepted only about 38 percent of the students who applied for admission. In 1989 there were 187 students enrolled in the institute.

Institute graduates receive the Secondary Physical Education Certificate. Graduates who earn a grade of "Very Good" on their certificate examination and complete two years of teaching are eligible for admission to the King Saud University College of Education as Physical Education majors.

As shown in Table 13-A, student enrollment in 1404 A.H./1984 A.D. was 17,391. Of these students, 11,102 were males and 6,289 were females. In 1414 A.H./1994 A.D. this figure increased by 264% to 63,367, of which 17,493 were males and 45,874 were females. The number of teachers also increased, by 69% over this eleven-year period, from 2,297 in 1404 A.H./1984 A.D. to 3,885 in 1414 A.H./1994 A.D. And of these teachers, 775 were Saudis and 3,110 non-Saudis as shown in Table 13-B. Table 13-A also shows that the number of schools decreased by 3%, from 201 in 1404 A.H./1984 A.D. to 196 in 1414 A.H./1994 A.D.

VII. SPECIAL EDUCATION

Special education was introduced into Saudi Arabia in 1958 when Sheikh Al-Ghanem, a blind man, learned the Braille system of reading and writing from an Iraqi man visiting the Kingdom at that time. Al-Ghanem introduced this new way of learning to a few other blind men, who were attending the general public school and to two sighted persons who had heard about the new system and were interested in learning more about it. This private effort lasted for about two years, during which time the system proved its usefulness as a vehicle for teaching the blind independent reading and writing. The Braille system was taught in one of the government schools at night, which allowed the blind students to continue attending their regular school during the day and also provided a place for Braille instruction. The government supported this private effort and offered the use of government space and materials. The great success of this venture prompted the government to formally incorporate special education into its programs.

In 1960, two years after those initial Braille classes, the Ministry of Education started a special education program and opened the first government-supported training institute for male blind students, the Al-Noor Institute in Riyadh. This was the cornerstone of special education program in Saudi Arabia. In 1964, the first school for the blind girls was founded. In the same year the first deaf school, the Al Amal Institute in Riyadh, was opened to provide education, training and care for deaf children. By that time, resources for the blind students had expanded to five institutes. The first specialized institute for mentally retarded children, Al-Riaih Institute, was opened in 1971.

In 1974, the Ministry of Education passed resolution No. 674/36/40 to upgrade the Department of Special Education to a General Directorate. It established three units to be responsible for the education of the blind, deaf, and the mildly retarded students. These three units are responsible for the preparation and execution of educational programs for each group, both male and female; monitoring educational progress and ensuring that the schools follow the established program. The department also plays a role in enlightening the parents regarding the benefits of special education for their children.

There has been a steady expansion of resources for the disabled students as new institutions were founded in different geographic locations according to the needs of each province. Schools for the handicapped have increased from one school in 1960 to 27 schools in 1987 and most recently to 54: 10 schools for the blind, 28 schools for the deaf and 16 schools for the retarded.

While Tables 14-A and 14-E below show the over-all increase or decrease in student enrollment, number of schools, teachers and classes for special education over an eleven-year period, 1404 A.H./1984 A.D. to 1414 A.H./1994 A.D.; Tables 14-B, 14-C, and 14-D provide information for each specific category under special education, namely: the blind, the deaf and the retarded. Schools for special education had the following over the same 11-year period: a decrease of 1 school or 10% for the blind, and increases of 12 schools or 120% for the deaf and 7 schools or 100% for the retarded. Increases in the number of special education students are as follows: an increase of 229 blind students or 79%, an increase of 1,327 deaf students, or 164%, and an increase of 1,559 retarded students or 341%.

Although the number of teachers for the deaf and retarded increased by 401 and 361, respectively; the number of teachers for the blind decreased by 159, from 427 in 1404 A.H./1984 A.D. to 268 in 1414 A.H./1994 A.D.

And while the Ministry of Education focuses its efforts on special education of the deaf, blind and mildly retarded children, it is the Ministry of Labor and Social Affairs that provides the very much needed attention to the physically disabled, severely retarded and multi-handicapped children.

The objectives of special education are to:

1. To discover each child's skills and abilities, in order to develop them through appropriate programs and activities.

2. To give children every opportunity for education and to help them achieve their highest potential.

3. To raise children with an awareness of Islamic teachings and morals.

4. To develop acceptable social behavior and prepare children for a stable life.

5. To provide stability for the disabled children and to provide needed medical, psychological and social care, and to help children become as independent as possible.

6. To prepare children for possible work in order for them to be productive and self-supporting members of society.

7. To educate the general public about disabilities and to foster greater understanding on how to interact with disabled children.

Three government agencies administer the different types of services for the disabled. While the Ministry of Education oversees educational programs for students of normal school ages, its General Secretariat of Special Education, under the directorship of the Deputy Minister of Education, develops the specific social and technical services required. The Ministry of Labor and Social Affairs supervises programs for older students beyond the normal school age and focuses on training and rehabilitation programs. The Ministry of Health provides integrated medical, psychological, and counseling services as part of its physical rehabilitation programs. In addition, the General Presidency of Youth Welfare provides a variety of sports, cultural, and recreational activities for the disabled.

A. The General Secretariat of Special Education

In 1962, the Ministry of Education established the first administration of special education which was responsible for the development and supervision of all special education programs. A decade later, in 1972, the administration was promoted to the status of Directorate General with several specialized departments.

The General Secretariat of Special Education, as it is now known, oversees planning and implementation of programs for the disabled students at all levels throughout the Kingdom. It formulates specialized policy and procedures, and offers technical assistance and training programs. The Secretariat also ensures that each local educational district has the proper facilities to accommodate the disabled students in that area.

The Educational Advisory Unit conducts ongoing research, field visits and evaluation of special education programs and related social services. It also reviews and updates special education curricula, textbooks and extra-curricular activities, and selects special equipment suited to the needs of disabled students. The unit is also responsible for improving teaching methods and providing teaching and guidance materials for educators.

The development and administration of educational programs for students with different disabilities is divided among three departments: the Educational Administration for the Blind, the Educational Administration for the Deaf, and the Educational Administration for the Mentally Retarded. The Center for Physical Therapy and Training cares for students of the special education institutes and offers physical and occupational therapy focused on the specific disabilities of individual students.

TABLE 14-A
Total Number of Schools, Students, Teachers and Classes for Special Education, for School Years 1404 & 1414 A.H.

SPECIAL EDUCATION	SCHOOLS		STUDENTS		TEACHERS		CLASSES	
	1404	1414	1404	1414	1404	1414	1404	1414
Blind	9	8	371	519	427	268	93	90
Deaf	10	22	1269	2134	286	687	135	233
Retarded	7	14	731	2016	168	529	95	201
TOTAL	26	44	2371	4669	881	1484	323	524

*Special Education is under the sole supervision of the Ministry of Education. but since 1414 the _____

Sources:
1. Ministry of Finance and National Economy, 1404 A.H.
2. Ministry of Education, Statistical Chart for School Year 1414 A.H.

TABLE 14-B
Total Number of Schools, Students, Teachers and Classes for the *BLIND*, by Boys and/or Girls, for School Years 1404 & 1414 A.H.

GENDER	SCHOOLS		STUDENTS		TEACHERS		CLASSES	
	1404	1414	1404	1414	1404	1414	1404	1414
Boys	7	8	290	519	—	268	93	90
Girls	2	—	81	—	—	—	135	—
Gender Unspecified	—	—	—	—	—	—	95	—
TOTAL	9	8	371	519	427	268	323	90

Sources:
1. Ministry of Finance and National Economy, 1404 & 1414 A.H.
2. Ministry of Education and General Presidency of Girls' Education Statistical Charts for School Year 1414 A.H.

TABLE 14-C
Total Number of Schools, Students, Teachers and Classes for the *DEAF*, by Boys and/or Girls, for School Years 1404 & 1414 A.H.

GENDER	SCHOOLS		STUDENTS		TEACHERS		CLASSES	
	1404	1414	1404	1414	1404	1414	1404	1414
Boys	6	22	807	2134	75	453	77	233
Girls	4	—	462	—	18	—	50	—
Gender Unspecified	—	—	—	—	—	234	8	—
TOTAL	10	22	1269	2134	93	687	135	233

Sources:
1. Ministry of Finance and National Economy, 1404 & 1414 A.H.
2. Ministry of Education Statistical Charts for School Year 1414 A.H.

TABLE 14-D
Total Number of Schools, Students, Teachers and Classes for the *RETARDED*, by Boys and/or Girls, for School Years 1404 & 1414 A.H.

GENDER	SCHOOLS		STUDENTS		TEACHERS		CLASSES	
	1404	1414	1404	1414	1404	1414	1404	1414
Boys	4	14	457	2016	34	338	56	201
Girls	3	—	274	—	134	—	35	—
Gender Unspecified	—	—	—	—	—	191	4	—
TOTAL	7	14	731	2016	168	529	95	201

Sources:
1. Ministry of Finance and National Economy, 1404 & 1414 A.H.
2. Ministry of Education and General Presidency of Girls' Education Statistical Charts for School Year 1414 A.H.

TABLE 14-E
Total Number of Teachers for Special Education
by Saudi and/or Non-Saudi, for
School Years 1404 & 1414 A.H.

NATIONALITY	BLIND		DEAF		RETARDED		TOTAL	
	1404	1414	1404	1414	1404	1414	1404	1414
S a u d i	363	166	85	267	34	175	482	608
N o n - S a u d i	64	16	201	186	134	163	399	365
Nationality Unspecified	—	86	—	234	—	191	—	511
T O T A L	427	268	286	687	168	529	881	1484

Sources:
1. Ministry of Finance and National Economy, 1404 & 1414 A.H.
2. Ministry of Education and General Presidency of Girls' Education Statistical Charts for School Year 1414 A.H.

B. *The Institutes of Special Education*

The Al-Noor Institutes for the Blind provide educational training and cultural programs in addition to full health, social and psychological care for sight-impaired boys and girls. The Institutes offer room and board for students whose families do not live within commuting distance. Sight-impaired students, whose vision is between 6/24 and 6/60 in the strongest eye or both eyes with the aid of corrective lenses, generally study in regular public schools which provide them with special health and social services.

The Institutes use the same grade structure and curriculum as the regular public schools for elementary, intermediate and secondary levels. Students who complete their secondary level education are encouraged to pursue further study at the university level and are eligible for government financial support and scholarships. There are also occupational training programs for older students that focus on manual skills such as weaving, rug making, manual and machine knitting, constructing cleaning equipment and home economics. In addition to the general curriculum, secondary level female students also learn child care and typing skills. Students are expected to be in the same general age group appropriate for regular public schools; for nursery, four to six years old; elementary, six to fifteen years old; intermediate, up to twenty years old; and secondary, up to twenty-five years old.

The Al-Amal Institutes for the Deaf provide educational and health-related programs for hearing-impaired boys and girls. Room and board are available to all students whose families do not live near the Institutes. There are three grade levels in the programs; nursery, elementary and intermediate. Hearing-impaired students enrolled in the intermediate section specialize in two technical fields chosen from typing, photography, printing, electrical wiring, manual and machine knitting, and tailoring.

Admission requirements for the Al-Amal Institutes specify that students be completely or partially deaf with a hearing loss of at least 80 decibels in one or both ears after treatment and the use of hearing aids. The students' ages must be consistent with the educational level for which they apply: for nursery, four to six years old; elementary,, six to twelve years old; and intermediate, twelve to twenty years old. The best qualified graduates from the intermediate level are eligible for government scholarships for specialized training courses in Great Britain. Further training at the post-secondary level is available to some graduates at specialized institutions in Europe and the United States, such as Gallaudet College in Washington, D.C.

Students with less severe hearing impairment --generally less than 80 decibels after treatment and use of hearing aids -- are served by special classes provided by the regular public schools. Not all schools have these classes, however, and some students must remain in the Al-Amal Institute until a special class is available in their local public school.

The Al Tarbiyah Al Fikriyah Institutes for the Mentally Retarded offer comprehensive educational and training programs, full health care and room and board for educable mentally retarded boys and girls. Special curricula are available at the nursery and elementary levels and are carefully adapted to the abilities and needs of students.

The more seriously retarded students who are classified as trainable are sometimes sent by the government to special training institutes in Egypt, Syria, Lebanon and Jordan. The most severely retarded who need complete physical care are enrolled in residential units run by the Ministry of Labor and Social Affairs where total health, social and psychological services are provided.

Students at the Al Tarbiyah Al Fikriyah Institutes must be in good health and do not have any other disabilities in addition to mental retardation. Students must have an I.Q. in the range of 50-75 and be between the ages of four and fifteen. Students who suffer from multiple disabilities which inhibit their full participation in the programs offered by the three special education institutes are generally enrolled in the school that serves the most severe handicap.

SPECIAL EDUCATION TEACHER TRAINING

In addition to studying their specific majors, teachers attend the special education classes that are provided. Initial courses are six months to two years in length. Some courses are offered in Saudi Arabia, such as the special education program in the College of Education, and the audiology program for speech and hearing specialists in the College of Applied Medical Science, both at King Saud University. The government sponsors teachers to attend those specialized programs that are only available abroad. Special education teachers are recruited from qualified public school teachers who wish to specialize in teaching the disabled and who have a minimum of three years experience.

Special education teachers are also required to take periodic short courses which present new teaching methods in their fields. The special education institutes also sponsor conferences and seminars that focus on specific issues, the new developments in the fields and advanced therapies available. Specially developed counseling materials are prepared annually to assist special education teachers and support staff.

Over the last two decades the special education programs in Saudi Arabia has grown into a system equipped to help the disabled students and their special needs. Institutes for the blind, deaf and mentally retarded offer educational programs and training opportunities that enable the disabled students to reach their maximum potential.

VIII. ADULT AND EVENING EDUCATION

The Ministry of Education and the other educational authorities give considerable attention to adult education. In 1975/76, an ambitious plan was launched to eradicate illiteracy in twenty years through four stages. (Ministry of Education, 1986-88, pp.36-37). The stages are:

a) The Initial Stage - The hope was to eradicate 20% of the illiterate population in the first five years, 1395/1396 -1390/1400 A.H. (1975/1976 - 1979/1980 A.D.);

b) The Expansion Stage - The hope was to eradicate an additional 25% of the illiterate population, 1400/1401 -1404/1405 A.H. (1980/1981 - 1984/1985 A.D.) and another 30% in the third five years, 1405/1406 - 1409/1410 A.H. (1985/1986 -1989/1990 A.D.);

c) The Third Stage - The hope was to eradicate 24% more of the illiterate population in the following three years, 1410/1411 - 1412/1413 A.H. (1990/1991 - 1992/1993 A.D.);

d) The Final Stage - The hope is to eradicate illiteracy among the remaining 1% of the illiterate population in the last year 1413/1414 A.H. (1993/1994).

Adult education programs were established throughout the Kingdom to help combat illiteracy. These programs were developed and are supervised by the General Secretariat for Adult Education under the directorship of the Deputy Minister of Education. Over 90 percent of adult education classes are coordinated by the Ministry of Education and the General Presidency of Girls' Education, and utilize public school facilities and teachers. National education policy requires all private schools to offer their share of adult education classes in order to qualify for government assistance. It further states that the major objectives of combatting illiteracy and adult education are: (Educ. Policy, pp.33-34)

1. To foster love and respect for God in the hearts of all citizens and supply them with necessary religious knowledge.
2. To teach reading, writing and elementary arithmetic.
3. To enlighten students about the general affairs of life and the development of their society.

The basic program teaches reading, writing and arithmetic up to the fourth grade. Students who complete the requirements of this program receive a Literacy Certificate. There is a standardized curriculum that is used in all adult education classes and the textbooks for this introductory level have been specially designed for adult students.

The next level of adult education is the follow-up course which continues education in reading, writing and arithmetic up to the equivalent of sixth grade elementary level. A Certificate of Completion of Elementary Studies for adults is awarded to its graduates. Intermediate and secondary level evening schools have also been opened by the Ministry of Education to expand opportunities for a broader range of students. As shown in Table 15-A below, there were 2,812 schools in 1404 A.H./1984 A.D. for adult education. This number decreased by 3% or 2,714 in 1414 A.H./1994 A.D. There was also a 16% decrease in the number of adult education students, from 138,378 to 115,988 in the same eleven-year period. There was a 54% decrease in the number of teachers, from 9,296 in 1404 A.H./1984 A.D. to 4,285 in 1414 A.H./1994 A.D. Table 15-C shows that of the total 4,285 teachers in adult education, 3,695 or 86% were Saudis and 590 or 14% were non-Saudis.

The period 1990-1992 saw efforts in revising the curriculum, taking into consideration the modern trends, the standard of the learners and the interaction of the subjects being taught. Adult education centers were provided with everything necessary to ensure the programs' success —facilities, textbooks, audio-visual aids, qualified and experienced teachers, and, most importantly, a proper atmosphere for learning. Also, financial rewards were given as incentives in learning.

Adult education does not end in combatting illiteracy. Adult education provides for the continuing education into the higher levels of education. Evening schools are made available throughout the country to enable male adults and those who work during the day to pursue their education and sit for the general examinations held by the Ministry of Education. They may continue their university study or use the certificates they obtain to improve their standard of living.

TABLE 15-A
Total Number of Schools, Students, Teachers and Classes for Adult Education, by Supervising Agency, for School Years 1404 & 1414 A.H.

SUPERVISING AGENCY	SCHOOLS 1404	SCHOOLS 1414	STUDENTS 1404	STUDENTS 1414	TEACHERS 1404	TEACHERS 1414	CLASSES 1404	CLASSES 1414
Ministry of Education	1443	1238	66023	45348	3628	—	3124	2499
Pres. of Girls' Educ.	1210	1356	58365	62402	5009	4133	4334	5358
Other Gov't Agencies	104	107	11762	7423	545	152	448	757
Private	55	13	2228	815	114	—	109	—
TOTAL	2812	2714	138378	115988	9296	4285	8015	8614

Sources:
1. Ministry of Finance and National Economy, 1404 A.H.
2. Ministry of Education and General Presidency of Girls' Education Statistical Charts for School Year 1414 A.H.

TABLE 15-B
Total Number of Schools, Students, and Classes for Adult Education, by Boys or Girls, for School Years 1404 & 1414 A.H.

GENDER	SCHOOLS 1404	SCHOOLS 1414	STUDENTS 1404	STUDENTS 1414	CLASSES 1404	CLASSES 1414
Boys	1553	1340	78554	51773	3587	3155
Girls	1259	1374	59824	64215	4428	5459
TOTAL	2812	2714	138378	115988	8015	8614

Sources:
1. Ministry of Finance and National Economy, 1404 A.H.
2. Ministry of Education and General Presidency of Girls' Education. Statistical Charts for School Year 1414 A.H.

TABLE 15-C
Total Number of Teachers for Adult Education by Saudi and Non-Saudi, for School Years 1404 & 1414 A.H.

NATIONALITY	1404	1412
Saudi	4486	3695
Non-Saudi	4810	590
TOTAL	9296	4285

Sources:
1. Statistical Year Book, 1404 & 1414 A.H.
2. Statistical Charts for School Year 1414 A.H., Ministry of Education and General Presidency of Girls' Education.

IX. OTHER TRAINING PROGRAMS

The Institute of Public Administration
The Institute of Public Administration (IPA) trains current and prospective civil service employees through full-time pre-service programs, in-service training programs and executive seminars. There are three branches of the Institute for males in Riyadh, Jeddah and Dammam and one branch for females in Riyadh.

Admission to IPA is highly selective. In addition to the educational certificate appropriate for a specific program, a written entrance examination and interview are required for admission. Graduates earn a Certificate of Completion in the program that they have selected.

Most executive seminars and in-service training programs require an Intermediate School Certificate. Pre-service programs require a six-week internship in a government office in addition to regular coursework, examinations and projects. Pre-service program graduates must also work for the government for a period equal to that of their training. The following programs require a Secondary School Certificate for entry:

- Banking -- two-year program;
- Electronic Data Processing -- a two-year program including a summer term, students must have certificate from secondary science division;
- Hospital Administration -- a two-year program;
- Library Science -- a three-year program;
- Personnel Studies -- a two-year program;
- Secretarial Studies -- a two-year program;
- Store Administration -- a two-year program.

Aside from the above, three pre-service programs that require bachelor's degrees for entry are the following:

- Banking -- a two-year program that trains students to work in banks or the Saudi Arabian Monetary Agency;

- Financial control -- a two-year program that trains students to work as auditors for the Ministry of Finance and similar government agencies;

- Legal Studies -- a two-year program that trains students to work as legal consultants in government offices. Graduates are ranked within the civil service similarly with workers with master's degrees.

Enrollment at the Institute of Public Administration in 1994 was:

LOCATION	STUDENTS	TEACHERS SAUDI	NON-SAUDI
RIYADH	12845	322	65
EASTERN PROV.	3244	27	11
WESTERN PROV.	4700	36	8
GIRLS'S BRANCH	3585	22	22
TOTAL	**24374**	**407**	**106**

The Military

Each branch of the military in Saudi Arabia -- Army, Navy, and Air Force -- has its own training academy or college. In addition, there is an academy for the National Guard which is the King Khalid Military Academy and another for police which is the King Fahd Security Academy. All these institutions require a Secondary School Certificate, personal interview and physical examination for admission. The programs lead to bachelor's degrees and are three years in length and coursework generally extends over nine months per year.

The Bachelor of Military Science is awarded to the graduates of the King Abdulaziz Military Academy in Riyadh (Army) which had 1,484 students in 1990-1991. The Bachelor of Naval Science is awarded to graduates of the King Fahd Naval College in Dammam (Navy) which had 471 students in 1990-1991. The Bachelor of Air Force and Aviation Technology is awarded to graduates of the King Faisal Air Force Academy in Riyadh (Air Force) which has a requirement of six months of English and six months of military orientation in its first year of program.

The curricula at these military colleges combine basic subjects such

---

*Source: Institute of Public Administration.

The curricula at these military colleges combine basic subjects such as Arabic, Qur'an, English, Mathematics, Psychology and Chemistry with extensive courses in Military Science. The three-year bachelor's degrees granted by the military academies are not evaluated consistently for transfer credit by Saudi Arabian universities. Umm Al-Qura University admits students with military academy degrees for graduate study and King Abdulaziz University accepts up to ninety semester hours of transfer credit. King Saud University, however, does not accept any transfer credit.

Health Care

Health institutes and nursing schools offer training programs for students who are interested in technical level positions in health care fields. The first health institute was founded in Riyadh in 1958 as a joint program with the World Health Organization. There are now more than twenty separate schools for male and female students that are supervised by the Ministry of Health. Health institute programs are at the secondary level and an Intermediate School Certificate is required for entry. The programs are three years in length and the students are generally between the ages of fifteen and twenty. These institutes train nursing technicians, x-ray technicians, laboratory technicians, health supervisors, surgical operations assistants, assistant pharmacists, assistant statisticians and nutritional assistants. Graduates from these programs receive a Health Institute Diploma. There are also three intermediate level nursing schools for females that offer a three-year program that leads to a Certificate of Technical Nursing.

The Institute of Diplomatic Studies

The Institute of Diplomatic Studies under the supervision of the Ministry of Foreign Affairs was established in 1979 (1399) with the following objectives:

1. To raise the standards of the employees of the Ministry of Foreign Affairs and other government agencies whose work is related to foreign affairs;

2. To conduct research and studies on international, Arab, and Islamic issues, and to publish them;

3. To organize conferences and seminars relating to diplomatic, political and international affairs.

The programs in this institute are aimed at preparing a core of diplomatic personnel who will be qualified to analyze current issues and changes in our contemporary world and to provide them with the experience, knowledge, and culture in order that they may possess practical and theoretical proficiency and qualification. The Institute has three (3) sections, namely:

1) Diploma Program in Diplomate Studies —

    —This program is for entry level diplomats and is two academic years in length;

2) The Proficiency Studies Session —

    —The program objectives are to provide new studies and to update information in terms of political, economic, legal and diplomatic issues.

3) Training Program for Wives of Diplomats —

    —The aim of the program is to expose the wives of diplomats to the cultures of different countries.

The Institute also has various annual and bi-annual publications such as:

—The Diplomatic Studies magazines;
—The Diplomatic magazine;
—The Saudi Studies magazines—
—The Annual Report

The Institute's enrollment in 1990-91 was 4,124 Saudis and 84 non-Saudis with 13 Saudi and 18 non-Saudi teachers. The number of diplomats' wives taking the training programs at the institutes in 1990-1991 was 721 all of whom were Saudis with 5 Saudi and 3 non-Saudi teachers.

Ministry of Telecommunications

The Ministry of Telecommunications provides training programs in the field of telecommunications. The two training institutes, one in Riyadh and the other in Jeddah, had the following enrollment figures:

Riyadh — 222 students and 98 teachers
Jeddah — 178 students and 95 teachers

X. CURRICULUM, TEXTBOOKS, AND SCHOOL FACILITIES

The rapid growth of the educational system in Saudi Arabia is reflected in the ongoing evaluation and development of the materials and physical resources used in the daily school experience. Some important issues and recent changes in educational resources such as curricula, textbooks, equipment and physical facilities used in the Kingdom's educational system are surveyed here.

Curriculum Development

The curricula used throughout the educational system in Saudi Arabia undergo a constant process of change and improvement in response to social and economic developments in the Kingdom, as well as international developments in technology. National committees, established by the Ministry of Education in 1984, are devoted to curriculum development and review, and advise the Educational Development Department of the Ministry. These committees study the subjects being taught in schools at different levels and deal with special issues such as adult education, measurement and testing, special education, audiovisual aids, and student guidance and counseling. There is close cooperation between the Ministry of Education and the General Presidency of Girls' Education on curriculum development, and experts from both agencies participate in the national committee activities.

There have been many innovations in curriculum development in the last several years such as the development of new mathematics texts for secondary education. Schools have been equipped with a variety of audio-visual media including television monitors, slide and overhead projectors, and school broadcasting facilities that have been integrated into the teaching of mathematics, science, and geography. Language laboratories have been built for the study of English and other foreign languages. School libraries have been converted into comprehensive educational resource centers stocked with books, reference works, newspapers, maps, posters, and films.

Special training courses have been developed to show teaching assistants how to use and produce a broad range of educational materials and media. In addition, two-week training courses have been designed to acquaint teachers with new educational technology. Longer training programs have also been instituted to keep teachers up-to-date on new directions in specific subjects such as mathematics, English, and science.

The General Presidency of Girls' Education has also coordinated several changes that have specifically affected girls' education. For example, new texts or methods for art education have been introduced into girls' elementary school grades 1-3. A new mathematics text and teachers' guide were developed for the third grade of secondary school. The English textbook used in the third grade of secondary school has also been revised. In addition, science and language laboratories have been installed in girls' schools, as well as audio-visual resources.

There have been several recent changes that affect adult education programs in Saudi Arabia. The administrative structure governing these programs has been reorganized to better integrate the efforts of professional educators from many institutions, including the Ministry of Education, the General Presidency of Girls' Education, Saudi universities and local school districts. A standard curriculum with specially developed textbooks is used throughout the Kingdom and all students must now take examinations. Also, data are now collected to track the registration, attendance, and graduation of adult education students, and these materials are considered a regular part of all statistics and studies on the Kingdom's educational system. Evening schools and home students have also been affected by changes in their academic school year which has been divided into two semesters, each of which culminates in individual subject examinations. The end-of-semester examinations are currently counted equally in evaluating students' work and are also used in making promotion decisions.

Textbooks

Committees at the Ministry of Education and the General Presidency of Girls' Education oversee the development of textbooks in every subject for all educational levels. Textbooks are generally written by subject specialists and an improved communication system now provides teachers and students the opportunity to contribute their feedback about how well individual books serve the everyday needs of the classroom environment.

Textbooks are updated periodically to reflect developments in different subjects. The textbooks used in Islamic studies, for example, which primarily cover the traditional religious texts and their interpretation, change very little over the years. Textbook materials in fields such as mathematics, science and social studies, however, are reevaluated regularly.

Similar textbooks are used by male and female students who also follow the same academic curricula. It is compulsory that private schools use the same textbooks and curricula employed in the public schools. The government provides textbooks to private schools free of charge. Supplementary textbooks are sometimes used by private schools for the extra subjects that are not available in the public schools such as when beginning English in elementary school or offering French as a foreign language.

School Facilities

Over the last two decades Saudi National Development Plans have provided for a massive program to improve the physical facilities of the educational system. This has included the construction and furnishing of new schools and the upgrading of existing schools. Most schools in Saudi Arabia are now furnished with science laboratories and appropriate equipment and supplies. Audio-visual media are fully integrated into the curriculum and schools are provided a full complement of equipment including slide projectors, televisions, video recorders, cassette and sound recorders. Many schools, from the elementary through secondary levels, produce their own media materials, such as educational videos illustrating a current subject under study that are broadcasted through the in-house closed-circuit television system. Some schools also have photographic equipment and photo-processing laboratories.

The government provides all schools with computers that are introduced to students beginning at the elementary level. Software in Arabic is abundant and specific programs are used in the teaching of Islamic studies, reading, mathematics, Arabic language and social studies. Software has also been developed for use with curricula covering different aspects of Islamic studies, including the Qur'an, Hadith and Tafsir.

These are but a few examples that illustrate the government's ongoing commitment of providing the best resources for the Saudi educational system. Improvements in curricula, textbooks, school facilities and other areas have resulted from careful planning that endeavors to match new ideas and technologies with the needs of Saudi students.

XI. CONCLUSION

This book, an overview of the educational system in Saudi Arabia, has shown the tremendous strides made by the Saudi government in the field of education. As the Kingdom presses forward vigorously onto the modern 21st century with other nations, there are still a number of problems to solve, systems to adopt and adapt, studies to undertake and countless avenues for improvement to choose from in redefining and refining education. Careful evaluations have to be made in addressing certain issues such as the apathy demonstrated towards the teaching profession, the negative attitude towards menial jobs, and others.

As more and more Saudi women take active roles in contributing to the development of Saudi mainstream society in the Kingdom, it is also imperative to expand the variety of fields of study for women, encouraging them to grow individually and collectively, offering them other professional opportunities besides teaching and nursing.

Saudi educators in the Kingdom are also faced with the big challenge of minimizing the number of school dropouts in line with the illiteracy eradication program. And, the question of educating the slow learners and the physically and mentally handicapped provides limitless challenges to creativity in education.

Lastly, it is hoped that education in the Kingdom of Saudi Arabia will be as dynamic as it should be, but without having to sacrifice the Kingdom's strong sense of heritage and tradition and deeply-rooted commitment to Islam.

XII. SELECTED BIBLIOGRAPHY

Al Kheraigi, Fatma Salem, *Special Education Development in the Kingdom of Saudi Arabia from 1958 to 1987*, Ph.D. Dissertation, Syracuse University, 1989.

Al Muslat, Zaid Abdullah, *Effort of the Kingdom of Saudi Arabia in Educating the Deaf.* Riyadh: General Secretariat of Special Education, n.d.

Al Rasheed, Mohammed A. and A. Al Sunbul, *World Perspective Case Descriptions on Educational Programs for Adults: Saudi Arabia.* Battle Creek, MI: Kellog Foundation, 1989.

Al Salloom, Hamad Ibrahim, *A Study Of The Relationship Of School District Size And Administrative Practices In Schools In Saudi Arabia.* University of Oklahoma, Ph.D. Dissertation, 1974.

Al Salloom, Hamad Ibrahim, *Tarikh Al Harakah Al Ta'limiyah fi Al Mumlakah Al 'Arabiyah Al Sa'udiyah: Tatawwur Al Tanmiyah Wa Al Idarah Al Ta'limiyah (History of Educational Development in Saudi Arabia: Development of Educational Administration)*, Book 1 Part 1, Second Edition. Riyadh: n.p., 1987.

Al Salloom, Hamad Ibrahim, *Al Ta'lim Al Am fi Al Mumlakah Al 'Arabiyah Al Sa'udiyah 1409/1988 (General Education in the Kingdom of Saudi Arabia).* Riyadh: n.p., 1988.

Al Sunbul, Abdulaziz, "ABE in Saudi Arabia." *Adult Literacy and Basic Education.* 9, no.3 (1985): 144-53.

Baltow, Abdullatif Mohammad, *A Historical Analysis Of The Saudi Arabian Ministry of Education's Policies Regarding Fathers' Involvement In The Schooling Of Their Children.* Michigan State University, Ph.D. Dissertation, 1983.

Dayil, Abdulrahman Sulaiman, *A Study To Identify Ways of Increasing The Enrollment of Saudi Male Elementary School Teachers in Teacher Training and Improving the Quality.* University of Idaho, Ph.D. Dissertation, 1978.

Directorate General of Special Education Programs, *Directory of Special Education in the Kingdom of Saudi Arabia.* Riyadh, 1981.

The Educational Administration of the Blind, *The Saudi Experiment in the Field of the Education of the Blind.* 1984/1985.

Faheem, Mohammed Eisa, *Higher Education and Nation Building—A Case Study of King Abdulaziz University.* Ph.D. dissertation, University of Illinois, Urbana-Champaign, 1982.

Fozan, Mohammed Ahmad, *Combatting Illiteracy In Saudi Arabia And The Problems That Face It.* University of Southern California, Masters in Education Thesis, 1980.

Fozen, Mishary Ibrahim, *Problems Confronting Public Education in Saudi Arabia.* University of Southern California, M.A. Thesis, 1980.

General Presidency for Girls' Education. *Statistical Chart, 1412-1413 A.H.*

General Organization for Technical Education and Vocational Training, *Technical Education and Vocational Training—Great Strides to a Prosperous Future.* 1989.

Gohaidan, Mohamed Soliman S., *Organizational Innovations in Developing Countries: The Case of Saudi Arabia.* University of California-Santa Barbara, Ph.D. Dissertation, 1981.

Hobday, Peter *Saudi Arabia Today*, St. Martin's Press. 1978.

Khateeb, Mohammed Shahhat, *Relating Technical Education to Industrial Manpower Requirements in the Kingdom of Saudi Arabia.* Ph.D. Dissertation, University of Southern California, 1985.

Manea, Azeezah A., *Historical And Contemporary Policies Of Women's Education In Saudi Arabia.* University of Michigan, Ph.D. dissertation, 1984.

Ministry of Education, *Development of Education in the Kingdom of Saudi Arabia, 1406-1408 A.H./1986-1988 A.D*. A Paper presented to The International Conference on Education, 41st Session, Geneva, January 1989.

Ministry of Education, *Development of Education in the Kingdom of Saudi Arabia, 1408-1410 A.H./1988-1990 A.D*. A Paper presented to the International Conference on Education, 42nd Session, Geneva, September 3-8, 1990. 1990.

Ministry of Education, 1992, *Development of Education in the Kingdom of Saudi Arabia,1410-1412 A.H./1990-1992 A.D*. A Paper presented to the International Conference on Education, 43rd Session, Geneva, September 14-19, 1992.

Ministry of Education, *Educational Policy in the Kingdom of Saudi Arabia*. 1978.

Ministry of Education, *Educational Statistics in the Kingdom of Saudi Arabia*. 1985-86.

Ministry of Education, *Educational Statistics in the Kingdom of Saudi Arabia*. 1984-85.

Ministry of Education, *Statistical Chart, 1412-1413 A.H.*

Ministry of Finance and National Economy, Central Dept. of Statistics. *Statistical Year Book, 1404 A.H.*

Ministry of Finance and National Economy, Central Dept. of Statistics. *Statistical Year Book, 1411 A.H.*

Ministry of Finance and National Economy, Central Dept. of Statistics. *Statistical Year Book, 1413 A.H..*

Ministry of Higher Education, *Statistical Index of Progress of Higher Education from 1969/70 to 1986/87.*

Ministry of Higher Education, *Statistics of Higher Education in the Kingdom of Saudi Arabia, 1990/91.*

Ministry of Planning, *Kingdom of Saudi Arabia—Fourth Development Plan*. 1985.

Ministry of Planning, *Kingdom of Saudi Arabia—Fifth Development Plan.* 1990.

Oliver, E. Eugene, *Saudi Arabia: A Study of the Educational System of Saudi Arabia and a Guide to the Academic Placement of Students in Educational Institutions of the United States*, Washington, D.C.: International Education Activities Group of the American Association of Collegiate Registrars and Admissions Officers. 1987.

Rasheed, Mohammed A. *Sources of Educational Goals in the Arab Gulf States,* Paper presented at the 33rd Comparative International Education Society Annual Meeting. Cambridge, Massachusetts, Marcch 31-April 2, 1989.

Rashid, Dr. Nasser Ibrahim and Dr. Esber I. Shaheen, *King Fahd and Saudi Arabia's Great Revolution.* U.S.A., 1987.

Royal Embassy of Saudi Arabia, *Saudi Arabia—Education and Human Resources.* 1989.

Sahabi, Abdulmalik, *Saudi Arabian Students In The U.S.: Their Attitudes Toward The Educational Policies and Practices In Saudi Arabia.* Kansas State University, Ph.D. Dissertation, 1987.

Saleh, Mahmoud Abdullah, *Development of Higher Education in Saudi Arabia.* Higher Education, 15, no. 1-2 (1986): 17-23.

Shakhis, Mohammed Abdullah, *An Empirical Investigation Of The Educational Leadership Styles, Attitudes And Needs In Saudi Arabia.* University of Tennessee, Ph.D. Dissertation, 1984.

Taibah, Ahmed Mohammed K., *Career Education: Assessment of Needs, Existing Educational Resources, And Practices In Saudi Arabia.* University of Southern California, Ph.D. Dissertation, 1988.

Towagry, Ali Mohammed, *Organization Analysis And Proposed Reorganization Of The Ministry Of Education Of The Kingdom Of Saudi Arabia.* University of Arkansas, Ph.D. Dissertation, 1973.